ALONE ON THE RIDGEWAY

A TALE OF TWO JOURNEYS BETWEEN AVEBURY
AND IVINGHOE BEACON

HOLLY WORTON

Alone on the Ridgeway:
One Woman's Solo Journey from Avebury to Ivinghoe Beacon

by Holly Worton

ISBN 978-1-911161-73-8 EPUB
ISBN 978-1-911161-74-5 paperback

Tribal Publishing Ltd.
Kemp House, 152
160 City Road
London EC1V 2NX

DISCLAIMER

Although the author and publisher have made every effort to ensure that the information in this book was correct at press time, the author and publisher do not assume and hereby disclaim any liability to any party for any loss, damage, or disruption caused by errors or omissions, whether such errors or omissions result from negligence, accident, or any other cause.

The information in this book is meant to supplement, not replace, proper walking and hiking training. Like any sport involving physical exertion, equipment, balance, and environmental factors, long-distance walking poses some inherent risk. The author and publisher advise readers to take full responsibility for their safety and to know their limits. Before practicing the skills described in this book, be sure that your equipment is well maintained, and do not take risks beyond your level of experience, aptitude, training, and comfort level.

Ultimately, only you are responsible for your own safety. Keep this in mind, especially when walking alone. Enjoy!

CONTENTS

PART III
PLANNING

RIDGEWAY
NATIONAL TRAIL

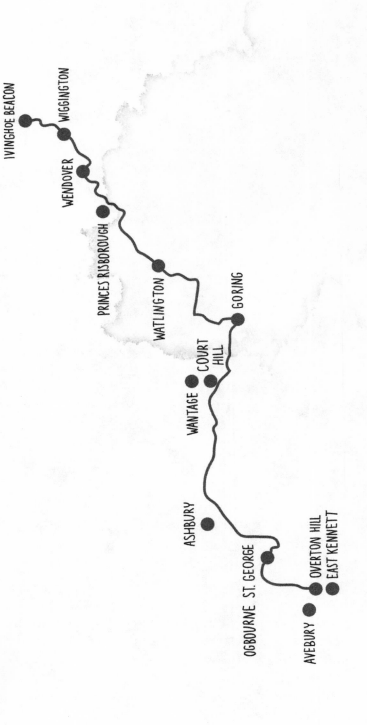

IVINGHOE BEACON

WIGGINGTON

WENDOVER

PRINCES RISBOROUGH

WATLINGTON

GORING

COURT HILL

WANTAGE

ASHBURY

OGBOURNE ST. GEORGE

OVERTON HILL

EAST KENNETT

AVEBURY

PREFACE

It's the year 2021 when I write this, almost five years after I first walked the Ridgeway in 2016. I've learned a lot since then: I've walked the Wey-South Path, and I've walked the South Downs Way and the Ridgeway a second time. On each journey, I was able to refine my training, my preparation, and my process of walking a long-distance trail.

After a fantastic second adventure on the South Downs Way in 2019, I was anxious to re-walk the Ridgeway in 2020. I was curious as to what it would be like. And I wanted to see what it was like to walk the trail in the opposite direction, ending in what is now one of my favorite places in the world: Avebury.

It's also the middle of one of the UK's lockdowns due to COVID-19. I've been getting outdoors for my daily exercise, either for a walk or a trail run. But it's been a long, wet, and muddy winter. And I'm ready for some longer outdoor adventures. I had originally planned to walk and camp along the Dales Way in March or April, but that definitely won't happen until much later in the year.

If you're in lockdown when you read this, I hope this book

gives you some ideas for new adventures once things open up. I also hope that you learn something from my experiences. I've been careful to share both the good and the bad. I include all of my mistakes so that you can avoid making them yourself. The Ridgeway is an absolutely magical adventure, and I hope you find it to be every bit as joyful as I did.

Holly Worton
February 2021

PART I

WEST TO EAST

INTRODUCTION

I published the first edition of this book almost a year after I walked The Ridgeway, my second National Trail, and my third walking adventure. At that point, long-distance walking had become a regular part of my life: it was something I planned into my annual calendar so I could make sure it would happen. Being alone out on a trail for several days in a row has always been a profoundly transformational experience for me. It's a time of relaxation and reconnection with myself, and I value it greatly. It's a great adventure.

This book was the third of my long-distance walking books, and I was so excited to release it and share my story. If you've read any of my other books, you'll have an idea of how much things have changed for me since I walked my first long-distance trail, the South Downs Way. In the epilogue for my first book, I wrote, "My experience on the Way was wonderful and horrible and also magical." It was anything but easy; in fact, I was surprised by how challenging it was.

On my journey along the South Downs Way, I seriously wondered on more than one occasion whether walking long-distance trails was for me. On the one hand, I loved the experience, but on the other hand, it was just so painful. I made many mistakes on my first journey, and I paid the price with a fair amount of discomfort. Fortunately, I decided to give long-distance walking another go by doing the Downs Link, a short 37-mile trail that stretches from St. Martha's Hill on the North Downs Way to the South Downs Way and beyond, ending at Shoreham-by-Sea in the south.

The Downs Link was such a different experience, and I loved it. I was able to make changes to how I approached the walk, taking into consideration some of what I'd learned while walking the South Downs Way, which made for a much more enjoyable adventure. I enjoyed the Downs Link so much that I walked it not just once in 2016 but twice. It rekindled my interest in long-distance trails, and it got me excited to walk the Ridgeway in August 2016.

One of the things that I relished about the South Downs Way was the feeling that I was in another world, somehow separate from ordinary reality and yet so close to home. The Ridgeway, a less famous National Trail than the South Downs Way, gave me an even more intense feeling of remoteness: 2016 was an unusually quiet year on the trail, and on one day, I walked for six hours and saw only four other people. The sense of peace and solitary passage through nature was delicious.

This quiet, remote feeling only serves to amplify the sensation of mobile meditation that I get when I'm out walking on my own: my mind goes blank as I put one foot in front of the other, advancing toward my final destination. I find it profoundly relaxing and deeply cleansing for my mind. My thoughts fade into the background, replaced with a deep stillness that is not usually present in my daily life.

In my first walking book, I shared the good and the bad, the beauty and the challenges of walking 100 miles. Most readers of Alone on the South Downs Way have told me that they enjoyed reading both the ups and downs of my walk, as it showed the full gamut emotions that I experienced along my journey. It was heartening to receive that feedback because when I reviewed one of my first drafts of the book, I was concerned that it was too negative and went too much into the painful details of each stage of the walk. Still, in the end, I opted to include everything I had written about my challenges: the good and the bad. After all, that was the truth of my experience.

Most readers understood that the book was my attempt to express the rollercoaster of emotions that comes with walking a long-distance trail for the first time. However, at least one reader found the book to be "anti-social, whinging and unfit," as one Amazon review warned. I mention this now, in the prologue, because this book is very much like Alone on the South Downs Way, in that I wrote the bulk of it in the evenings of my journey, while enjoying a pint of Guinness after having dinner. That means that you'll be hearing the full range of ups and downs that I experienced on the Ridgeway—though thankfully, there were more ups than downs on this National Trail.

This book will give you a good idea of how I've grown and evolved as a walker since my journey along the South Downs Way. I share the mistakes I made so that you can avoid them yourself. Having walked 100 miles once before, the 87-mile Ridgeway felt much more doable. I was a more confident walker on this trail, and I'm a more confident writer in sharing my experience.

The other thing I was concerned about when writing my first walking book was the slight woo factor in Alone on the South Downs Way: I pulled oracle cards for each day of the walk, and I shared messages from my Akashic Records readings. I was terrified of putting those details into print and sharing them with the world, but one reader told me that those details were what separated my book from other walking books out there, which gave me a bit of confidence.

And that's why I've decided to unleash a bit more of my woo in this book: I'll be sharing the story of how I channeled a new set of spirit guides as I walked the Ridgeway. This channeling isn't a significant part of the book, so if you're not used to hanging out with nonphysical beings, that's fine—be aware that the Richards (yes, that's what they call themselves) do make an appearance on each day of my journey.

I sincerely hope you enjoy your adventure along the Ridgeway with me: the emotional, the practical, and the woo. It was a memorable experience, and it's a very, very special trail. It's my wish that it inspires you to get outdoors and into nature a little bit more—whether for a day hike or a long-distance trail.

Let's get started!

DAY 0: AVEBURY AND THE SURROUNDING AREA

9.3 MILES (15 KM)

My 2016 Ridgeway walk began in late August, the week after I returned from my second Downs Link adventure. It felt strange to be packing my backpack for another long-distance trail less than a week after I had returned from the Downs Link, but that's how things had worked out in my calendar. I hadn't noticed that I had booked the Downs Link weekend so close to the Ridgeway walk; I had chosen the first available weekend I had that summer. I was excited to experience that trail again so that I could get the book out and share my journey with others.

I had initially wanted to walk the Dales Way in 2016, as I'd never walked in the north of England, but after the previous winter's torrential rain and flooding, the trail was damaged, and I wasn't confident in my ability to navigate the various detours along the path. I considered Glyndwr's Way, a National Trail in Wales, but after reading Andrew Bowden's book *Walking with the Last Prince: Following Owain on the Glyndwr's Way*, I realized that the trail was much more challenging than I was looking for. I was still a bit apprehensive about doing another weeklong walk, and I wanted to be sure that I chose one of the easier trails. I read Andrew's book *Rambling Man Walks The Ridgeway: From Overton Hill to Ivinghoe Beacon*, and I immediately decided on the Ridgeway as my National Trail of choice for 2016.

It ticked all the boxes. The Ridgeway was short (at just 87 miles, it met my desired trail length of 100-mile maximum), it was not too challenging in terms of hills, and it was full of historical sites. I had become fascinated with pre-Roman British history after returning to the Devil's Jumps, a place along the South Downs Way known for its collection of Bronze Age tumuli, or burial mounds. The Ridgeway seemed like it would satisfy my interest in ancient sites: it has two long barrows, multiple hill forts, and more tumuli than I could count.

That was how I found myself planning a Ridgeway walk for August 2016. When I walked the South Downs Way, I learned just how challenging long days were for me. I had walked the 100 miles of the South Downs Way in eight days, so I decided to stretch the 87 miles of the Ridgeway out in the same amount of time, adding a ninth day in the beginning to explore the area around Avebury. I figured that would make it easy enough for me.

I came to think of this first part of my journey as Day 0 since it wasn't technically a part of the Ridgeway. Day 0 was a long one, though thankfully, there wasn't much walking than my previous weekend on the Downs Link. This short day meant that I had plenty of time to warm up for my National Trail adventure. I clocked in just over 9.3 miles (15km) of walking by the time I reached my B&B at 6 pm that afternoon.

The day started well: a leisurely drive to Avebury with my husband. We parked in the National Trust car park at Avebury and wandered around the stones for about an hour before he got in the car and headed back home. It was a nice transition to the solitude of my walk, but I felt strangely reluctant to say my goodbyes—as if I didn't want to let go.

I had enjoyed our wander around the Avebury stone circles, and I felt slightly apprehensive about being on my own, which was unusual for me. One of the things I relish the most about my long-distance walks is that I do them alone. They provide such a deep level of mental rest, despite the physical activity. Yet something was holding me back from getting excited about my journey ahead, and I didn't understand what it was.

I had a list of things I wanted to do in Avebury before heading toward my accommodation for the evening, but it was 1 pm when we said goodbye, and I wasn't sure I'd have enough time for it all. Despite being a tiny village, Avebury is home to the largest stone circle in Europe. The surrounding area boasts several ancient sites: tumuli (round barrows or burial mounds), a massive human-made hill, and an impressive long barrow. This region was not only well-populated back in the Bronze Age, but the people were hard at work constructing these ancient sites that remain thousands of years later.

If you're considering walking the Ridgeway, I recommend that you add an extra day before the start of your journey to explore Avebury and the surrounding area. I was so grateful that I did so. At first, I had considered getting an extra early start on my first day of the Ridgeway and making it a long day by exploring Avebury and then starting the trail. I later thought the better of it and decided that would be too much in one day. Instead, I tacked on the extra day before the start of my main journey. Avebury has since become one of my favorite places in England, and I've returned many, many times since my first visit.

After watching my husband pull out of the car park toward home, I headed straight for the Barn Gallery of the Alexander Keiller Museum to get a ticket for the 2 pm guided tour of the stones. I also wanted to ask about the Avebury Manor House and Gardens. It was summer, so there was a fair amount of tourist activity, but I quickly bought my ticket for the stones and booked an entry time for the Manor—free with a National Trust membership card.

If you visit the Avebury area, the name Alexander Keiller will come up quite frequently. Keiller was a Scottish businessman and amateur archaeologist who was fundamental in preserving and studying the Avebury site. He was the heir to his family's marmalade business, and he purchased a total of 950 acres (3.8 square kilometers) in Avebury to preserve and excavate the site. Thanks to Keiller, we know as much as we do about the stone circle, and it is thanks to him that the site is so well preserved. Many of the stones were sadly knocked down and broken up during the Victorian era to build cottages in the village, but Keiller stopped this and prevented further destruction of the circle.

Keiller eventually sold his property in Avebury in 1943 to the National Trust, and in 1986, the site was designated— along with Stonehenge—to be a UNESCO World Heritage Site. The National Trust now manages the stone circles, the Alexander Keiller Museum, and the Avebury Manor and Gardens. This means that the museum, manor house, and gardens offer free admission to all National Trust members, though the stone circle is always free of charge for everyone to visit (unlike Stonehenge, which is pricey for non-members).

After getting my tickets, I settled down for a quick lunch on a rustic log bench before the stone circle tour began, and then I went to meet the tour group. It was a small gathering of about ten people, plus the guide. The tour was fantastic, just under an hour and a half, and was surprisingly informative. I had thought there wouldn't be much to say about such an old site— after all, there are no records of how it was built or why—but the guide had so many stories about Keiller's restoration of the site that I was thrilled that I had booked the tour. It was well worth both the £3 fee and the time spent.

There are usually at least two or three tours a day in the

summer, with one or two each day throughout the rest of the year, and I highly recommend you plan to join one of the group tours. It adds meaning and context to the stone circles. Otherwise, you're just wandering around looking at a bunch of standing stones.

Near the end of the tour, it began to drizzle. It had been overcast most of the morning and early afternoon, varying between a cloud-covered sky and occasional bits of sun. Now, it looked like it might rain for the rest of the afternoon, which made for an ominous start to my journey.

The man who worked the ticket desk at the museum had been kind enough to offer to let me stash my hefty 36-liter pack behind his desk while I went to the Manor House. After the tour, I rushed back to drop off my pack at the Barn Gallery and then I headed over to the Avebury Manor in time to make my scheduled entrance to the house. I huddled under a small overhang to get out of the rain as I waited to enter. A volunteer greeted everyone at the door, explained a little bit about the house, and then let everyone run off to explore by themselves. The house was set up for visitors to do a self-guided tour, with laminated information sheets in each room.

Avebury Manor & Garden is a Grade I listed early 16th-century manor house located on the site of a former Benedictine Priory built in the 13th century. The house was privately occupied until recently when it was refurbished in 2011 for the BBC One series The Manor Reborn. The following year, it opened to the public. Unlike most historical residences, visitors are encouraged to touch the furnishings and the objects in each of the rooms, which were refurbished to represent different periods in the house from the 16th to the 20th centuries.

As you might expect, the manor house is reputed to be haunted, by not one but four ghosts, according to Keith Wills, author of Haunted Wiltshire. If you're fascinated by this kind of thing, check out the book before visiting Avebury, so you know what—or who—to look out for. And if you're a bearded man, be especially aware of the White Lady, who may tap you on the shoulder when you're in the manor house gardens. Don't say I didn't warn you.

Unfortunately, I was unaware of the manor house ghosts during my visit, and I didn't bump into any of them while I was there. After my supernaturally uneventful tour of the house, I saw that it was drizzling a bit harder by the time I exited the Manor, and I rushed through the gardens on my way back to the Barn Gallery to retrieve my pack. The rain had no intention of ceasing, so I hid under an eave of the barn to protect myself from the wet as I pulled my waterproof jacket from my backpack. It was warm out, but I was a bit damp and started to feel a little chilly.

I spent some time wandering around the different parts of the circle once more—which were now beautifully devoid of tourists due to the rain and the late hour. Then I decided to head off toward my final three attractions of the day: West Kennet Avenue, Silbury Hill, and West Kennet Long Barrow. They were all on my way to that night's accommodation—The Old Forge in East Kennet.

I had bought the Trailblazer guide to the Ridgeway, written by Nick Hill, the same publisher as the guidebook I had used for my South Downs Way walk. These excellent guidebooks include everything you need to know about planning your hike, including where to stay and how to split up each day of your journey. They also have hand-drawn maps for each stage of the trail. I like to highlight the routes in different colors before my departure, marking the route itself in yellow, water taps in blue, interesting nature spots in green, historical sites in pink, and other essential landmarks in orange. This color-coding makes it easier for me to spot things at a glance when on the trail, and I enjoy making the maps a bit more colorful.

The Trailblazer guide includes a series of shorter walks

around the Avebury area, the most interesting of which—if you're planning to spend a day in Avebury before starting the Ridgeway—is the "Walk Around Avebury." This route is a short, 6-mile (10 km) circular walk that perfectly fits into a day in Avebury, allowing you to take in the surrounding archaeo-logical sites. If you're not walking the Ridgeway and just want to spend a day in Avebury, I'd recommend that you walk the full circular trail. Yet if you are walking this National Trail, I suggest that you walk the western portion of the route and stay the night in East Kennett, which is situated right on the circular, just a short distance from the start of the Ridgeway.

The beauty of this circular walk is that it takes in the following sites: Avebury and its museums, West Kennet Avenue, Silbury Hill, West Kennet Long Barrow, the village of East Kennet, the Sanctuary, and the first portion of the Ridgeway before turning off down Green Street to return to Avebury. That's why it's the perfect route to explore the area, whether you're walking the Ridgeway or not.

I hadn't taken the time to calculate how long it would take me to reach my B&B in East Kennet that afternoon, but I esti-mated it would be about two hours. I stopped under some large beech trees at the edge of the Avebury stone circle for a quick snack of water and nuts. The top of my pack was starting to get wet from the light rain, so I pulled out its integrated rain cover to protect it from getting soaked before getting back on my feet to head down the little mound. I emerged from under the trees' shelter and went through a small gate, carefully crossing the street and entering West Kennet Avenue on the other side of the road.

A prehistoric site located just beyond the Avebury stone circles, West Kennet Avenue, was originally a 1.5-mile (2.5 km) path flanked by standing stones, running between Avebury and The Sanctuary, another ancient site located just across the street from the start of the Ridgeway. An estimated 100 pairs of standing stones originally lined the avenue. However, most of them have since fallen or are missing (or have been repurposed for building cottages). Some of the missing stones were marked by Alexander Keiller by small concrete pillars, and it's easy to imagine just how impressive the avenue would have been as you walk down it today.

The rain was no more than a drizzle as I walked down the wide path, which was flanked by this odd combination of stones and concrete markers. There were still several standing stones along the way, and they were now surrounded by a herd of black and white cows, who didn't seem to mind my presence as I walked carefully amongst them. A quiet country lane sat beyond the stone avenue, on my left. I passed through the gate of one field to head straight on through a second gate. There, I saw a fingerpost sign indicating that Silbury Hill was to the right (this was where I was heading), and a stone circle could be found to the left, just 1/4 mile away (150 m).

I looked off in that direction and saw only fields and a line of trees, but it was such a short of a detour and I didn't want to pass at a chance to visit yet another stone circle, so I turned around and exited the gate I had just passed through, then crossed the road and walked down the narrow path alongside a field. I kept going for about ten minutes until it was clear there was no stone circle to be seen. The only place it could be was at the top of a small hill that sat straight in front of me, but that was much further than 1/4 mile.

I decided that heading up to the hilltop was too much of a detour to make, especially considering there were no guarantees I'd find anything once I got up there. It was getting late, and it was wet. I turned around and backtracked to the fingerpost sign, where a family of walkers asked me about the stone circle. I told them that I hadn't found anything, and they decided to avoid the detour themselves.

A couple of months later, I searched for this mysterious

stone circle on my first return visit to the Avebury area. I retraced my steps and saw nothing, so I continued straight on, alongside fields, until I reached the top of the hill I had seen on my first visit to the area. Still, no circle. I walked up to a pair of tumuli, where I rested in the quiet shade before returning down the hill.

On my way back, I encountered a woman walking her dog, and I asked if she knew about the stone circle. She confirmed that there was no circle left, just a single standing stone near the road, which I could see alongside the trail if I looked out for it. I kept an eye out as I retraced my steps back toward the road, and I eventually saw the lone standing stone, the last remains of the old stone circle. I was satisfied to have solved the mystery of the stone circle, yet sad that it had been destroyed, like so many other ancient sites in the area. If you decide to do the circular walk around Avebury, it's probably not worth the detour to see the standing stone, though it will only take you five minutes off the main route.

Back on the main path, I walked up the slope of Waden Hill, along a wide, open green path. I passed two small hawthorn trees on the right, one of which was covered in multi-colored ribbons. The rest of the hillside was open and grassy, devoid of other shrubs or trees.

As I reached the top, I could see the conical shape of Silbury Hill down the other side, looming up from the flatness of the surrounding countryside like a giant green volcano. The trail headed straight down Waden Hill toward Silbury, then turned right and followed down the right-hand side of a dry riverbed before turning left over a little bridge and around the other side of Silbury.

Silbury Hill is a human-made prehistoric grass covered chalk mound, and at 131 feet (40 mt.) is the tallest prehistoric human-made mound in all of Europe. Experts still debate its original purpose, and excavations have not yet solved the mystery of why people felt the need to invest an estimated 18 million hours of work to build it. That's equivalent to 500 people working for 15 years. Even if you adjust the estimate to 250 people working for 30 years, that's still a massive investment of time and energy. Between Silbury Hill and the large stone circles at Avebury, it's clear that the ancient people in the area were a hardworking bunch.

It was at this point that I remembered my commitment to channeling some new guides. During a coaching session the previous week with Lisa Wechtenhiser (http://lisamw.com/), a new set of spirit guides appeared. They called themselves the Richards (I kid you not), and there were four of them. They had asked me to connect with one of them each day for the first four days of my journey, after which I should rest a day and then reconnect with one of them each of the last four days of my trip.

Before I get into my relationship with the Richards—which began on this day of walking around Avebury—let me explain a little bit about what spirit guides are. They are nonphysical entities, energies, or beings who can serve as guides, protectors, and teachers. They can be the spirits of people we once knew in this lifetime or previous lifetimes; they can be angels or be ascended masters. In a nutshell, they're nonphysical beings who are here to help us.

Yeah, I get it. This spirit guide thing sounds a little weird. You might believe in guides, or you might not. But The Richards were my guides as I walked The Ridgeway in 2016.

At the time, I was not an experienced channeler, as some of my friends were, and as Lisa is. I'd been doing it for a few years at that point, but I still second-guessed myself. It's not something that came easy to me, mostly because I didn't practice it as much as I wanted to. Let me be honest: channeling is a bit weird. It's not something that the vast majority of people do, even though we all can do it.

Back in August 2016, I was still not entirely at ease with my channeling. It seemed all fine and good for other people in my life to channel, but when I started hearing voices in my head— yes, I know how that sounds—that gave me guidance and support, that was a whole different story. Only once had I channeled verbally (that's when you allow a guide to speak through you, using your voice), and that was with the help of a friend. On most occasions, I would hear the messages in my mind, writing them down as they came through.

For some reason, I decided that day to start channeling verbally, allowing the words of Richard 1 to come through my voice. I planned to make notes later so as not to forget the message that I received. It was the first time I had verbally channeled while walking, and it felt a bit weird. The words came through haltingly, at times repeating themselves rhythmically. But it was all very practical and coherent.

When the four Richards first connected with me during my session with Lisa, they told me that they each had a message for me, something to give me and that these four elements would support me like the four legs of a table. I would receive one message from them every day for four days, and then I would rest; later, I'd revisit one of the Richards every day for the final four days of my walk.

I later regretted not recording my voice as the guide spoke through me on the first day, and I rectified that later. From my notes, I can share that the overall theme of the first message I received from Richard 1 was peace: peace of mind and the space to achieve it.

I was told that I needed to trust myself when channeling. That it was easier for me to verbally channel because it made it easier to trust myself. Hearing the words out loud somehow made them more real than hearing voices in my head. Because let's be honest: aren't we all a little afraid of hearing voices in our head? I know when I'm channeling because the messages I receive are spoken in a style that's not mine. I know that is comes from something outside of myself, but I'm also very much aware of how crazy it all sounds to someone who's not into this.

A friend of mine, Cara Wilde (http://carawilde.com/), is an experienced channeler and teacher of channeling, and her voice often takes on a different tone and accent when she channels her guides. I always liked this about her because it was easy to tell when she was speaking and when her guide was speaking. I wanted the same for myself and my guides. However, Richard 1 knew this, and it was evident that they would not give me a strange accent because I needed to learn to trust. When I fully trusted the channeling process, they might give me a different voice or accent. By doing the opposite of what I wanted, they would show me that I had grown as a channel and trusted myself and the process.

As I continued along the trail that wound its way around Silbury Hill, which was muddy and dotted with dark-colored slugs, Richard 1 informed me that I needed to slow down, like the slugs. I needed to rest. To relax. This was all part of his peace of mind message. "Peace and space," he said.

I felt a bit tired of the channeling as I walked, probably because it was a new process for me. I thanked Richard 1 for the message and disconnected from him, focusing once again on the walk itself. There were exceptional views of Silbury all down the trail's left-hand side, which came out in a small car park. I wandered down a short path that led to a viewpoint of Silbury Hill, where I read an information board, then backtracked and turned left down the busy A4 road. There was a narrow sidewalk that went alongside the road and a grassy green path next to that. I chose the green trail, which looped around the other side of Silbury, with the hill to my left.

The sidewalk eventually ended on my side of the street, so I crossed to the other, continuing down the road until I reached the turnoff for West Kennet Long Barrow. I passed through a metal gate and stopped briefly at an information board, which I read. I learned that West Kennet Long Barrow is one of the longest of this type of barrow—the name for a raised grave, or elongated tumulus—in Britain, at just under 330 feet (100 mt.) long. It's yet one more example of what the area's hardworking former residents managed to achieve, and experts estimate that it took just under 16,000 hours of work to construct.

I continued down a straight path, past a large old ribbon-filled oak on my left before the trail went over a little stream, then through another gate. The footpath turned to the left and passed by another old oak— also adorned with ribbons— where I turned right and started up another golden hill toward the long barrow. The trail was flanked on both sides by fields of grain.

It was late in the day, and the weather was still unpalatable for most tourists, which meant that no one else was headed up the hill, save for a solo person climbing up ahead of me. I passed two small groups of people coming down the hill toward me. When I reached the long barrow, the man ahead of me had already left it, and I had the ancient site all to myself.

West Kennet Long Barrow consists of an elongated mound with a very elaborate entrance made up of imposing standing stones. The barrow was remarkably well restored: you can enter its five chambers and walk around inside. I passed around the large stones that once sealed the barrow entrance and stood at the opening. It was completely dark inside and refreshingly cool. Three baby birds chirped anxiously from a small crevice in the stones to the left of the entrance. Their mother swooped in to feed them, and they quieted as I entered the barrow.

Turning on the small flashlight on my phone, I shone its small beam into each of the chambers to make sure that I was alone. I didn't want to be startled by the presence of an unexpected visitor, and I didn't want to interrupt anyone who was already in there. There was a slight incense smell, and there were small offerings of flowers and feathers in the main chamber at the end. The energy was strong and beautiful in the barrow, which surprised me, considering that I was all alone in a dark, damp place that had once been a burial chamber to at least 46 people. It's the kind of place that some people might think was a bit creepy.

I could tell, however, that this was an exceptional place. As I explored each of the five chambers, I realized that I wanted to spend more time at this ancient site. Unfortunately, I was tired and damp. I was anxious to arrive at the place I was staying for the evening, which was just a half hour's walk away in East Kennett. I knew that I wanted to stay longer at the long barrow, but I didn't have the energy to appreciate it fully, so I decided to continue onward to East Kennett.

I made the decision to retrace my steps the following morning to return to the long barrow. My journey on Day 1 would be a short one at just nine miles, and backtracking to West Kennet would only add an hour's walk onto the day's journey. It didn't really make sense to head back the next day, but I wanted to see the long barrow once more before starting out on the Ridgeway.

By the way, you may have noticed the inconsistency in spelling of Kennett and Kennet. There is a local custom of spelling the more modern villages of East and West Kennett with two Ts, and the ancient sites with just one. I have respected this in the telling of my journey.

As I exited the barrow and started back down the trail, I saw a family approach with small children. I was thankful I had decided to return rather than be interrupted by them while I was in the barrow. I felt a strong desire to be alone at the site. I descended the small hill, turning off to the right once I reached the bottom, toward my B&B in East Kennett.

It was still drizzling, and my legs were beginning to get soaked. I hadn't bothered to pull on my waterproof trousers, and my walking trousers were relatively thin. The trail had surprisingly little mud until that point, so I was still reasonably clean—just wet and uncomfortable. I knew I was close to my B&B, so I didn't bother to get out my waterproof trousers. Instead, I forged onward. I walked down a trail along the left side of a field, crossed a quiet lane, and continued through another field. The path curved around to the right, ending at a fence, where I climbed over a stile and headed down a dark, tree-lined trail that was pure mud.

There was no way to avoid it. The path was narrow and consisted of puddles and deep mud, which squelched under my feet as I walked. The trail eventually came out onto a paved road, where I turned right down a quiet country lane. I hoped The Old Forge was close, and I was relieved to see it just as I came around a bend. I was grateful to have arrived, and I was looking forward to a hot shower and shelter from the rain.

A teenage girl soon came to greet me at the door, and she showed me where to leave my muddy boots before leading me upstairs to my room, which had a private bath located just down the hall from my room. I asked about nearby dining options and found out that the local pub was closed for dinner on Sundays. She phoned another pub that was slightly farther away, and we discovered that it was also closed.

The only option for dinner would be to take a taxi to Marlborough, which I didn't like. After such a quiet day in the Avebury area, hopping in a car and going to a large town didn't appeal to me at all. I decided to stay in, have a quiet evening in my room, drink copious amounts of tea, and snack on some nuts that I carried in my pack. That sounded much more satisfying.

I settled in for the evening, taking a hot shower and carefully rinsing the mud off my trouser legs in the bathroom sink. I carefully washed out the rest of my clothes so they would be ready for my walk the day after tomorrow. The B&B was so pristine and lovely that I was terrified of muddying up my room, but I managed to clean my clothes and keep my room spotless.

I planned to follow the same laundry code as I had on my South Downs Way walk: bring two sets of shirts, sports bras, socks, and underwear, and wash them each evening, hanging them off the side of my pack the following day to dry in the sun. My system had worked perfectly on the South Downs, and I hoped it would work on the Ridgeway, weather permitting.

The Old Forge is one of those very organized B&Bs that give you a form to fill out with your breakfast and lunch order. After my shower, I completed the form detailing what I wanted for breakfast and for my packed lunch, then I took it downstairs and left it on a table near the entrance for the hosts to find. Returning to my room, I snacked on some nuts, made a mug of hot chocolate in my room, and devoured the biscuits on my tea tray before going to bed. It was not the most nutritious dinner, but it was satisfying, especially after such a wet afternoon.

I was excited to return to West Kennet the following morning. It felt strange to retrace my steps and revisit the site, but at the same time, it seemed like the perfect prelude to my official kickoff to the Ridgeway. To make that happen, I wanted to get an early start the following day. It would only be an extra hour's worth of walking, plus whatever time I spent at the long barrow, but I didn't want to feel rushed. I set my alarm to allow enough time to get ready before breakfast and got ready for bed. As usual, on my walks, I fell asleep quickly and slept deeply.

DAY 1: EAST KENNET TO OGBOURNE ST. GEORGE

9 MILES (14.5 KM)

I woke up before my alarm, which had become a habit on my walks. This makes perfect sense to me. I've read that it's common not to sleep well the first night in a new place because the brain doesn't fully rest—it's still adjusting to its new location. Unfortunately, on a walking holiday, every night is spent in a new place. Yet, I had gone to bed early: just after ten, which meant that even though I'd had a restless night of deep sleep broken up with some tossing and turning, I had managed to spend nine hours in bed with the lights out.

I turned on the kettle to boil water for a cup of tea and then did my morning meditation exercises as I waited for 8:00 to come around, which was the time I had requested breakfast. I went down a few minutes early and met Leslie, one of the hosts, who indicated the place at the table he had set for me. He brought out tea, and later my breakfast, and then his partner Laura came out to ask what sandwich I wanted in my packed lunch.

The Old Forge offers a variety of cooked breakfasts, not just the standard full English, and I had chosen egg and smoked salmon on a muffin, which was delicious. The lunch they packed for me was large, and I knew it was more than I'd be able to eat on my walk that day: sandwich, crisps, fruit, chocolate bar, and a juice box. After a typical heavy B&B breakfast, I usually ate light when out on the trail, so I knew it would last me for at least a couple of meals. Despite all the walking I'd be doing, I couldn't eat a full cooked breakfast and a big lunch.

After breakfast, I went upstairs to organize all my things in my pack, fasten it all up, and head downstairs to leave. The day was overcast, but it wasn't supposed to rain. I'm obsessive about checking the weather when I'm walking a long-distance trail, and I had reviewed the forecast just after waking up. I was hopeful that the day would be a dry one. After saying my goodbyes, I carefully put on my muddy hiking shoes, which had dried overnight into a crusty mess, and I headed out the door, back in the direction I had come from the evening before. Once out on the road, I stomped my feet to loosen the dried mud on my shoes.

I retraced my steps first down the road, then the muddy trail (which was still a mess), along the narrow tree-lined path, then alongside the fields until I was back on the wide, open track that led up the hill to West Kennet Long Barrow. I had picked some white hogweed flowers along the way, which I planned to leave in the large chamber of the barrow, where I had seen other offerings the previous day. I wasn't sure why I was doing this, but it seemed the right thing to do. As soon as I entered the barrow, the three little birds began chirping, and their mother once again swooped in with a meal. My arrivals at the barrow seemed to coincide with their mealtimes.

There was much more light in the barrow than there had been on the previous afternoon. It was not long after 9:00, and light streamed into the chambers from the small circular skylights above. I beamed my weak flashlight into each of the chambers to confirm that I was alone, then I left the flowers in the largest chamber. I sat down in one of the smaller ones near the right-hand side of the entrance to have a quiet moment alone in the barrow. There was still the faintest scent of incense from the day before and the same powerful yet lovely energy I sensed. I didn't understand what I was experiencing, but I knew it would become a meaningful place for me.

After some minutes, I got up and sat in the corner of the largest chamber. The soft morning light shone in from above, illuminating the flowers I had brought and a smaller bunch of yellow flowers and a sprig of wheat tied with a red ribbon. It was mid-August, and Lughnasadh had recently passed, and I assumed the offering of grain marked the celebration of the pagan harvest festival. The chamber was cool and damp, and a large sarsen stone to my right was moist with water that had dribbled down its front.

I sat in silence until I heard movement at the entrance: a photographer had arrived. I stood up to give him some time to photograph the barrow alone. I walked out of the opening, then up and all around the outside of the barrow. As I came full circle and approached the entrance once again, I saw that the photographer had finished and was on his way down the hill. I returned to the barrow and sat for several more minutes in a different corner of the main chamber. It was the darkest one, and once my eyes had adjusted to the dark, I could see just how well the skylight illuminated the rest of the chamber.

I was so comfortable, and I enjoyed the energy so much that I wanted to stay longer, but I knew I had a long walk ahead of me. It was just nine miles from the start of the Ridgeway to Ogbourne St. George, but I had made the half-hour detour back to West Kennet, and I still had to get back to East Kennet where I had stayed the night before, and then onward to the start of the Ridgeway. It was a quarter to ten, and it was time to be on my way. I knew that I could always return if I wanted (the site was less than two hours' drive from my home), and I have: since that first visit to the long barrow, I've gone back many times. It's become a special place of rest and reflection for me.

I retraced my steps once again: down the wide, open trail, through the fields, down the tree-lined path, through the muddy trail, and back on the road into East Kennet. I saw a church sign and headed down a quiet lane to find Christ Church, built in 1864 on the site of a 12th-century church. I went inside to look around, then quickly explored the church-yard before returning to the main road. I was still conscious of time, and I didn't yet need a break from my walking.

Continuing down the quiet road, I reached the fork where I was supposed to turn left and double back on my path toward the Ridgeway. The paved road soon turned into a narrow trail headed up through trees, over a bridge that carried the trail across a little creek, then up and out onto the busy A4 road. I could see the start of the Ridgeway ahead, just across the street. The Sanctuary, another ancient site, was located to the left of the trail, and I walked through the gate to explore it.

The Sanctuary sits on top of Overton Hill, just across the street from the official start to the Ridgeway. An early version of the site consisted of six concentric timber rings, erected around 3,000 BCE. Ancient people later expanded it into two concentric circles of standing stones. Unfortunately, it was destroyed in the 18th century, and the rings are now marked only by concrete posts. After the impressive sites of Avebury, Silbury Hill, and West Kennet, The Sanctuary is a bit anticlimactic. Still, it is said to have been an important site in ancient times, and it makes for a historic start to the Ridgeway.

After exiting the Sanctuary gate, I carefully crossed the road and paused at the dark brown sign marking the Ridgeway's start. My long-distance journey finally felt like a reality, and my stomach fluttered with excitement. At the beginning of the Ridgeway, in a field to the right side of the trail, sat three tumuli. I could see a fourth mound further down the field.

There were several "hedgehogs"—tumuli, that had been planted with trees—off in the distance. The guide at the Avebury stone circles had explained that the locals gave them that name due to their spiky appearance in winter when the trees were leafless. It seemed incredibly disrespectful that people had planted trees on top of these ancient burial mounds —but then, these were probably the same people who had destroyed the Avebury stones to use them for construction.

I walked onward through the small car park toward one of the information boards at Overton Hill, perusing the trail's map and description. I was excited to be starting on another new path. The sense of adventure and exploration of the unknown was thrilling.

Despite it being mid-August, the morning air was brisk. It was official: I was ready to go, and I started on the Ridgeway. I was alone, save for a man who speed-walked past me, with no pack on his back and nothing but a folded piece of paper in his hand. I couldn't imagine where he was planning on going like that. Was he a farmer? He didn't look at all like your usual hiker. I looked back and saw a small group of people further behind me, just exiting the Sanctuary and about to cross the road toward the Ridgeway. It appeared they were heading my way.

The Ridgeway was broad and straight and well signposted; it was impossible to lose my way. The trail was wide and deeply rutted, flanked by grain fields on either side, and it rose steadily uphill onto the ridge. A farmer in a field on the left side of the trail was busy moving bales of hay around on a tractor.

The wind whipped my clothing around on my pack, and I noticed I was missing a piece. I stopped, backtracked until I found it, then resumed my journey. I had passed several people during my detour: first a couple, then a small group of women. By the time I got back on track, they were no longer visible in the distance. I never managed to catch up with them that day;

perhaps they had turned down one of the many side trails that crossed paths with the Ridgeway, or maybe they were walking much faster than I. The morning's walk had been marked by detours—one planned, one unplanned—and I was hoping the rest of the journey would be straightforward. Although it was summer, and the days were long, I always worried (unnecessarily, of course!) about reaching my evening's destination before nightfall.

A gate to the right of the trail marked the entrance into Fyfield Nature Reserve, and I continued straight on, sticking to the Ridgeway. Parts of the track were level, but in some regions, the Ridgeway consisted of a series of four or five narrow rutted tracks that ran unevenly, up and down. It was a bit tiring in parts, and it was hard to keep an even pace on the path.

I passed one runner heading in the opposite direction, then a woman on a cycle. Despite the number of people I had seen when I first started the day, it was a quiet Monday morning on the trail. I had set out on the Ridgeway at precisely eleven, though I had been out walking since I left The Old Forge at 8:45 that morning. I continued until I saw a small bench on the left side of the trail—the first I had seen that morning. I stopped for a break and to eat some of my lunch.

I opened up the cheese and tomato sandwich and ate the entire thing. The juicy tomato had made the bread a bit soggy, and I knew it wouldn't last much longer. I was very thirsty, and it felt like the water I'd been drinking wasn't doing much to quench my thirst, so I opened the box of orange juice— even though this is something I rarely drink. It tasted amazingly delicious for a boxed juice, making me wonder if I needed to re-think my customary choice of walking beverages (water). I always walked with a pouch full of water in the summer and a flask of hot tea in the winter, but perhaps I needed to add a sugary fruit juice or electrolyte drink in the hotter months. In retrospect, electrolytes would probably be the better choice, but I enjoyed that box of cheap juice like never before.

I chose not to air out my feet during my break, which I knew was a risky move. I had learned on my Downs Link walks that taking my shoes off and changing my socks was the best way to prevent blisters in the hot summer months, yet I was always reluctant to do so. I was often just too lazy, so I decided to risk it, even though it was only the first day of my walk, and I still had several more to go.

It was a chilly morning, and though my feet were already a little tired, they weren't yet hot, and I resolved to let them cool out on my next break when it would surely be hotter. I continued on the trail, which turned into a stony path before heading up Hackpen Hill and across a quiet road with a car park on the other side. In 1838, a large horse figure was cut into the chalk of the hill. I had seen it from the road as we drove to Avebury the morning before. I debated about heading down the hill to see the white horse but chose to keep going instead.

Further down the trail, a small opening in the fence led to one of the hedgehog barrows, and I ventured in to see what one looked like on the inside. The perfect circle of the tumulus was covered with trees, dotted all over its surface. Unfortunately, I could see that the trees had disturbed the original rounded dome of the tumulus, as its surface now flowed up and down unevenly between the trees. The hedgehogs may be pretty from a distance, but the trees had destroyed the rounded natural form of such an ancient monument. They were yet another example of how locals had disrespected these old historical sites.

The trail curved gently around a bend, and I could see Barbury Castle looming off in the distance. It looked quite impressive, and I was looking forward to exploring its grounds. I was thankful that the Ridgeway went straight through the site because I wasn't too keen on another detour that afternoon. I was starting to feel tired, and it was only my second day of walking.

Barbury Castle is an impressive Iron Age hill fort, located right on the Ridgeway, with spectacular views. The II-acre fort is ringed by double ramparts, with ditches between them. There are entrances at both ends of the fort, which allow the Ridgeway to pass straight through it.

The Ridgeway sloped down a hill, then continued across a quiet lane and up the side of the old hill fort. A father and son on cycles approached me from behind, and I held the gate open for them to go through. The father cycled slowly up the steep hill, and his son got off to walk his bike up. I didn't blame him. I was thankful to be walking and not cycling—that seemed like a much more difficult way to undertake this journey.

When I reached the top, I could see there were several other people at the site. I decided to climb up to the highest ridge and walk around the right-hand side of the circle. The Ridgeway went straight through the middle of the hill fort's ground level, and I would have a much better view from up above. The narrow path continued all around the ridge of the rampart and sloped down on both sides.

I clicked along with my poles until I reached the other end of the hillfort, where the Ridgeway cut through to continue onward. I climbed down off the rampart and entered the hill fort's grassy green circle, where I sat down, taking off my shoes for a long rest. I knew I was close to Ogbourne St. George, my destination for that evening, but I wasn't quite sure how much I had left on the trail. According to my guidebook, it could be anywhere from 90 to 130 minutes, which seemed much longer than I had anticipated. I had initially estimated I would arrive at about 4:00 that afternoon.

I decided to keep an open mind and mentally prepare myself for arriving anywhere between 4:00 or 5:00. I was tired, and it had been an excellent decision to rest at the hill fort. The

Ridgeway was almost devoid of benches, with just one so far on the trail that day, where I had stopped to eat my sandwich. The only other benches I found were near the Barbury Castle Country Park's car park, just beyond the hill fort. The Ridgeway lacked in benches—clearly this trail is meant for moving, not resting.

I got up, walked out of the site, and headed toward the park's public toilets. I was looking forward to the privacy of a toilet rather than having to worry about someone surprising me by the side of the trail, but they were dark, dirty, and disgusting. After using them begrudgingly, I realized that I preferred the uncertainty of the outdoors, which seemed cleaner than the dark, damp toilets.

The Ridgeway continued out down a dirt path to the right of the entrance to the car park, then down an unpaved road. A large van approached from behind me, and I jumped off the trail so he could pass. He asked me if I knew the road's condition further ahead, and I replied that, unfortunately, I didn't. The road was dotted with large, water-filled potholes and didn't look like the best route for a large van. He said he'd give it a try and continued.

Almost immediately after, the Ridgeway made a left turn through a fence and continued downhill, on an open grassy track, with fields to either side. There were excellent views ahead: expansive stretches of rolling hills. The trail curved down and to the right, continuing along Smeathe's Ridge before passing through a gate with a cattle grid to its right. I stopped to eat the bag of crisps that had come in my packed lunch. I wasn't hungry, but I felt like I needed some salt, so I obeyed my body's signal.

From there, I continued down the trail before stopping at a broken fingerpost sign. There, the trail forked in two, and the Ridgeway appeared to continue down to the left. The route had been well signposted until now, and I wanted to be sure of the

correct path before I continued on my journey. I passed
through a gate and saw a man uprooting large bunches of
yellow daisies—ragwort—and collecting them in piles. I wasn't
sure whether he was the landowner looking to remove the
wildflowers or if he was taking them home to transplant in his
garden. It was like a massive foraging expedition. It seemed he
was pulling them up, root ball and all (an illegal act, if he wasn't
the landowner). I greeted him, and he ignored me. Perhaps he
was, after all, a wildflower thief.

It was time to check in with the Richards once again. Once
the flower burglar was safely behind me, I began verbally channeling, asking to connect with Richard 2. His message: patience
with myself. This time, I recorded his words.

"Patience with yourself," Richard 2 said, "will allow you to
make mistakes and feel okay about them. When you allow
yourself to make mistakes and feel okay about them, that
means that you will be able to take risks more easily. And when
you take risks more easily, that will help you to grow things that
you want to do in your business and grow your business more
quickly in the way that you like. You have been taking risks this
year, but you could take more." I received specific messages
about two business friends and the advice to get back in touch
with them and suggest a joint venture.

It felt like the right time to close off the channeling for that
day, and I put away my phone, which I had been using to record
the message. I passed a fenced-in reservoir to my right, and the
trail soon transformed into a leafy green tunnel of trees, the
first shady bit I had walked through that day. I would quickly
learn that this was typical of the western half of the trail: wide,
open byways with very little shade. The Ridgeway came out
onto a road, where I quickly turned right before heading back
onto a shady trail once again. A fingerpost indicated that while
the Ridgeway continued straight down on that tree-lined path,
the way to Ogbourne St. George was down the road to the left.

As this was the village where I would spend the night, I followed the sign and turned left off the trail.

I continued walking down the road, which wound down and around through a residential neighborhood full of pretty little thatched cottages. After walking for ten minutes, I worried that I had missed my B&B. I stopped to see if I had a mobile signal and used it to find my accommodation on Google Maps. It felt like I was in the middle of nowhere, and I couldn't believe the village was so large that I hadn't yet arrived at my B&B. Yet it was located just five minutes from where I had stopped, a total of fifteen minutes from the Ridgeway, down this quiet residential road.

I soon found it: The Inn with a Well, which looked a bit like a tired, old motel from the outside. Marley, the inn's dog, barked at me as I entered the car park, and I walked straight inside the pub to collect the keys to my room. I was tired and sticky with sweat, and all I wanted was a shower and a cup of tea after a long day on the trail. I was not disappointed in my room.

My room was spacious and, most importantly, the bathroom was fitted with a heated towel rack, which meant that I could wash and dry my clothes overnight. The discovery of a heated towel rack in my room is always a joyous one. I had learned from my long-distance walking adventures that this was one of the essential features of a B&B because it allowed me to dry my clothes quickly and safely, rather than risking loss or ineffective drying by hanging them on my pack. I took advantage of this and washed out my walking pants, which had become covered in mud on my walk back to the West Kennet long barrow that morning. I put on my evening clothes—a light, summery t-shirt dress—and relaxed in the chair with a cup of tea as I filled out my breakfast and lunch request form as I waited for the restaurant to open for dinner.

I was impressed by how organized the Ridgeway B&Bs

were. On the South Downs Way, just one B&B had forms to fill out for my breakfast and lunch requests. It was so much more practical, and it made ordering meals so easy. Once I had relaxed and recovered from the walk, I headed across the tiny car park and over to the pub for dinner.

The Inn with a Well gets its name from a well set into the restaurant floor, just inside the pub's entrance. The owners had installed bulletproof glass to provide a safe cover for the well, allowing guests to stand on top and look down the 30-yard shaft of the well, which is lit from the inside. I settled in for dinner and a pint of Guinness and typed up my account of the day's journey, occasionally lookin up to watch the pub's dog Marley wander in and out.

As I wrote, I saw the couple who had passed me at the start of the day. They entered and sat at a table in the corner. I listened in on the conversation with the waitress as she asked about their walk. They were also walking the full length of the Ridgeway, but they would be doing much longer days than I and thus finishing sooner.

I finished my pint of Guinness as I completed the day's writeup. I made the short walk back to my room, where I went to bed early, tired from the day's adventure and excited about the rest of my journey. Today was just the first day of eight on the trail, and so far, I was satisfied with my decision to walk the Ridgeway.

DAY 2: OGBOURNE ST. GEORGE TO ASHBURY

10.2 MILES (16.5 KM)

I finally managed to have a good night's sleep but was woken up before my alarm by the shrill voice of a toddler coming down the stairs outside my room with his family. I could hear them shushing him, but he was young and didn't understand the importance of being quiet before 7 am. I rolled over and immediately went back to sleep, and before I knew it, my alarm sounded.

After getting out of bed, the first thing I did was to check my clothes that I had left to dry on the towel rack, and I was thrilled to see that they were completely dry. If only all B&Bs nearby National Trails had towel racks for walkers to dry their clothes! (See how excited I get about such a simple detail?) I made a cup of tea to drink as I got dressed and then headed to the pub for breakfast.

Once again, I had been pleasantly surprised to see different breakfast options, other than the usual full English (not that I have any complaints with a full English breakfast, but I do enjoy having options). The night before, when filling out my meal forms, I had ordered eggs royale, once again opting for smoked salmon with my breakfast. The sandwich I had ordered for lunch was smoked salmon and cream cheese, and later that evening, I ordered a salad with grilled salmon for dinner. I realized that I had an unusual craving for salmon, and I wondered if I needed some fish oil, even though I had been taking supplements for the past couple of months.

Breakfast was served promptly, and the owner handed me my packed lunch before I went back to my room to do my morning meditation exercises. It was much like the previous day's lunch: a sandwich, crisps, a homemade cookie, orange juice box, and an apple. From what I had seen so far, the Ridgeway B&Bs were particularly good at packing a full lunch for walkers.

After finishing my morning exercises, I packed everything up and checked out of The Inn With the Well. I quickly walked the fifteen minutes through the village back to the Ridgeway, confident now that I knew exactly where I was going. It was busier this Tuesday morning, with cars passing me as I walked, but it was still quiet enough to make it an easy walk down the street.

The day was forecast to be hot and sunny, reaching 28 degrees (84° F). I had plenty of water in my pouch, and though I was grateful that it wouldn't be raining, I was also wary of the heat and sun. It reminded me of my week on the South Downs Way when I had sunny skies and record high temperatures of up to 39 degrees (102° F) on one day.

The trail was shady and tree-lined as it went down a stony path, then turned to come out through the village of Southend, which seemed to consist entirely of thatched cottages, including the more modern homes. The Ridgeway came out onto the A346 road, which I crossed before continuing down the path.

At this point, I should have passed the first of two water taps along the route that day. According to my guidebook, it was located just outside Elm Tree Cottage, but because I had the idea that both water taps were farther down along in my journey that day, I completely missed the first one. Though I might add, it wasn't marked with a sign—or perhaps I was just lost in thought as I walked. On my second Ridgeway walk, I saw the water tap—it was located not on the trail itself but was a tap on the side of someone's home. No wonder I didn't see it!

The good thing was that I had just started my day, so I had more than enough water with me for the first part of my walk. I was experimenting with carrying less water on my walks. Water was the heaviest item in my pack, and on previous trails, I had grown accustomed to starting the day with a full pouch of water—2.5 liters, which made my pack quite heavy. By carrying less water on the days I knew there would be water taps, I could lighten the load in my backpack a little. Fortunately, the second water tap of the day was hard to miss, and I was able to fill up my water bladder in the afternoon.

The trail crossed an old railway line—now converted into the 7.5-mile (12 km.) long Chiseldon and Marlborough Railway Path—then went under an old railway bridge. From there, it climbed through a tree-lined path up a hill. Then it crossed a road before continuing onward, steadily uphill. The trail was quiet that Tuesday morning; I had only passed two dog walkers along the way. One of them was kind enough to put the leash on his dog as soon as he saw me, even though it appeared friendly. Sometimes it seemed that the owners of the most well-behaved dogs were the most conscientious ones, while the owners of the dogs that growled and barked at me seemed oblivious to their dogs' behavior. I was always wary of crossing paths with an off-leash dog while walking; I never knew how they would react.

The Ridgeway climbed steadily, a bit more steeply than before, until it crossed another road and continued onward. The track was quiet, open, and sunny, with few trees alongside the trail. The morning was already hot, and I knew it would only get hotter as the day went on. My guidebook indicated that this portion of the trail was very muddy during wet weather, but mud was not an issue on this sunny day, and, luckily, my shoes stayed dry.

The trail curved slightly to the left before crossing a quiet street, which appeared to head toward Ogbourne St. George. So far, every road I had seen that day went toward the village, which made me feel like I hadn't traveled that far since departing my B&B that morning. The path was open, with excellent views of the trail I had walked along the day before off to my left. It was fascinating to see, from a distance, the hill I had come down after leaving Barbury Castle. Open fields of grain that had already been harvested lay to the right of the path I was on today. Most of the fields I was walking by were wheat.

The Ridgeway was still very quiet, with no walkers or cyclists passing me in either direction. The path entered a shady, tree-lined area with open fields on the far side of the trees. There, it split into two: a narrow trail for walkers on the left and the standard byway for walkers, cyclists, riders, and vehicles on the right. I kept on the wide part of the trail, as the walkers' path seemed a bit sunnier, and I had no desire for more sun than I already had on the wide track.

I passed another quiet country lane that headed toward the old, abandoned village of Snap to the right. Snap is unique because it wasn't abandoned until 1914, after reaching its peak of 41 residents in the 1851 census, most of whom were employed by local farms. Shortly after it became a ghost village, it was used for military training in World War I. I chose to avoid the half-mile (1 km.) detour to Snap since there wasn't much to see these days.

After crossing the road, I once again had the narrow footpath option to the left or the wide byway to the right. I kept with the shady byway since no one else was around anyway—

or so I thought. A runner came up silently behind me, startling me as he passed and continued on his way. I was so surprised to see another person on the trail that I jumped and yelped. I felt a bit silly about my reaction. At the same time, I was worried that I had been so out of touch with my surroundings. It was easy to lose myself as I walked.

Despite my previous day's success, when I had recorded my channeled message, I lazily connected with Richard 3 and began channeling without recording. My notes are, unfortunately, a bit disjointed from this portion of the channeling. He said something about progression 1-2-3-4, which I remember to be that the messages of the four Richards were coming in order, progressing from 1 to 2 to 3 to 4 and that each message would build on the previous one. The overarching message from Richard 3 had to do with financial stability.

He spoke of setting goals and of paying off credit cards. He said that it was vital for me to be very aware of my money situation; that I should always know precisely what was going on with my finances. I tended to put my head in the sand sometimes, so I wasn't surprised to hear this message. Richard 3 urged me to "put it all in the money app" (he was referring to an app that I used to track income) and for me to calculate the number of clients I needed to bring in to pay off debt and to visualize it all: the process of both bringing in the clients and paying off the debt. He reminded me that "energy/money flows where attention goes" and that if I wanted to bring in more income, I needed to focus on money.

Richard 3 reminded me to allow myself to focus on all the things I needed to learn and not to get distracted. He also advised me of the importance of doing gratitude work, which I had once done daily. I resolved to make this a more regular practice.

Once again, the path crossed a quiet country lane and continued. I approached a small group of trees on the right-hand side of the track, offering their shade to a large, fallen tree whose trunk had been cut into large pieces. As I hadn't seen any benches yet that morning, I figured this was the best I'd find to rest on, and I took off my pack and sat down for a break.

After I had rested a while, enjoying the shade, I stood up, pulled on my pack, and admired the view across the trail. I could see Swindon off in the far distance, but between the path and the large town, the landscape consisted of farmland and rolling hills in various shades of green and gold.

I turned to walk on and almost immediately saw a bench sitting among a small plantation of trees—the only one I would see on the Ridgeway that day. I had grown so accustomed to the lack of places to rest on the trail that I had taken advantage of the fallen tree trunk for my break, but if I had just continued walking a couple of minutes onward, I could have rested on a proper bench. I felt tempted to sit back down to take advantage of it, but I decided to continue.

I followed the trail, which began to head slightly uphill once more. I could see that it was opening up once again to go through golden fields of harvested wheat. There was no shade in sight ahead of me, and while the views were gorgeous, the day was getting increasingly hotter. I took a long drink from my water tube and forged on ahead.

The Ridgeway route for vehicles had veered off to the right, and I was on a narrow grassy footpath that climbed steadily alongside fields of short golden stalks that had already been harvested. Higher up on the hill, I could see a massive piece of farm machinery shining bright red on the horizon. The upper parts of the field boasted long grain waving in the breeze, waiting for harvest time.

A large herd of horses grazed on the right-hand hillside, and a surprising number of them were white. This was the first herd of horses I'd seen on the Ridgeway, in fact, the only horses outside of some stables I'd passed through the previous day.

Livestock on the Ridgeway so far consisted only of cows, and there weren't many of them. The fields were mostly grain.

As I approached the top of the hill, I saw a bit of shade alongside the trail, and I pulled off my pack, sitting down on the grass and taking out my packed lunch to eat my bag of crisps and drink the box of orange juice. Much like the day before, I was craving both sugar and salt. As I crunched through my bag of salty crisps, a farmer drove by on a tractor, and I waved to him. He seemed surprised to see someone sitting alongside the field, hidden in the shade, and he waved before continuing.

I got up, made a quick pit stop in the long grasses, and stood back up to continue my journey. I could see that I was approaching Liddington Castle, another Iron Age hill fort, and though the Ridgeway didn't pass directly by it, there was a permissive footpath that led to the outer ridge of the fort. I wanted to see it, and I walked straight on past the Ridgeway turnoff to the right and down the permissive footpath toward the hill fort, which was well signposted.

The path reached the end of the field, passed through a gate, then turned left toward the hill fort. I walked through uneven grassy fields that were slightly difficult to walk on, making it evident that few people opted to take this detour. It was no more than a ten-minute journey from the Ridgeway to the edge of the hill fort, and I ambled along the outer rim before scrambling down the steep hillside and back up the other side to the inner rim, where there were an old OS trig point and a plaque that showed which cities were in each direction.

If you've ever done any amount of walking in the UK, you'll have seen the Ordnance Survey's trig points. They're a series of concrete pyramidal pillars used to create maps using a triangulation system: when they were first installed, it would have been possible to see at least two other trig points while standing at one of them. This is often no longer the case, as the trig points were first built in 1936, and vegetation has changed since then, often blocking the view to the other locations. Still, I find them strangely fascinating, and when I come across one, I usually try to find the other points off in the distance. So far, no luck.

Despite my sun hat, my head felt hot. I wished there was a stream somewhere along the trail to wet my head and cool off, but of course, there was none. It was very, very dry on the Ridgeway that day. Every stream I had passed so far had been waterless, nothing more than a plant-filled line of mud. It was hard to get enough water out of my water pouch to wet my head, and I didn't want to waste my drinking water, especially since I was trying to travel light. Water is heavy, and I was carrying just what I would need, and a little extra.

I saw an empty one-liter Evian bottle next to the OS trig point, and I picked it up, tucking it into my pack to fill up at the much-awaited water tap. I planned to use the water bottle to cool off my head throughout the day. I couldn't remember the last time my head had been so hot, and the idea of wetting my hair was very appealing.

From there, I scrambled back down the inner rim and back up the outer edge. I continued along that rim until I reached an opening and walked inside it to the center of the hill fort. It was much like Barbury Castle in form, but not as well maintained, and there were no information boards. It was sad; it seemed like it was the forgotten historical site of the trail. Surely, something could be printed on a sign, but it seemed like no one cared enough to do so. Perhaps it was too remote and too inconvenient to access.

Given the heat, I decided not to explore any further, and I retraced my steps back toward the Ridgeway. As I walked, I could see a couple tromping ungracefully through the wheat field toward the hill fort. As they reached the permissive footpath, they climbed over the fence and headed in the direction of Liddington Castle. They were out walking without packs, and they had no water that I could see. I wondered if this visit to the hillfort were a spontaneous decision for them, as they seemed very unprepared for the excursion. We greeted each other as we crossed paths, and I turned down the correct permissive footpath to return to the Ridgeway. I wasn't sure how they had missed the proper trail, which was well sign-posted, but I felt bad for the farmer that they were barging through the previously pristine field of wheat.

Once I returned to the Ridgeway, it headed downhill between golden fields with giant rolls of straw bales dotted throughout. The trail was a vast, chalky track that passed by a World War II pillbox nestled amongst a clump of trees off to the left. Pillboxes are concrete and brick guard posts dotted throughout the English countryside. About 28,000 were built in 1940 as part of the anti-invasion preparations for World War II, and only a third of them survive today. There are plenty in the Surrey Hills, where I live, but this was the first one I'd seen so far on the Ridgeway—and indeed, it would be the only one I would see along the trail.

The path continued downhill alongside a field of harvested wheat. A cyclist passed me, going in the opposite direction. We greeted each other. A Land Rover turned off the road ahead of me, headed up the Ridgeway byway toward me, then abruptly turned off and drove swiftly across the field of wheat, possibly to avoid passing the cyclist and me on the byway. I hoped it was the farmer; despite the field having already been harvested, it didn't seem right to drive straight through it.

It was here that the Ridgeway, which up until this point had been a beautifully remote and historical trail, turned left down the busy B4192 road that fortunately had a narrow green verge that was wide enough to walk on. I knew from my guidebook that it soon turned right down another road, and though I

assumed it turned down a quiet rural path, it was a horren-
dously busy road that only had a very narrow verge to walk on
for some parts of it. Other stretches of the road were so tight I
had to walk in the street and hop up onto the little verge when
a car came by. This busy road was in stark contrast to everything I had seen since the start of the trail.

The Ridgeway soon crossed a bridge over the busy M4
motorway. Fortunately, trees were lining one side of the road,
and they provided much welcome shade in the heat of the
afternoon. The road was jarring and stressful, but it was shady,
unlike the more remote portions of the trail. I eventually
reached the crossroads where The Burj was located. This
Indian restaurant was the only sign of civilization on the
Ridgeway that day, save the busy road I had just walked down. I
waited for three large trucks to pass me on the road; then I
crossed over.

The Burj was deliciously air-conditioned and felt like an
oasis in the scorching afternoon heat. I walked up to the bar
and ordered a large bottle of sparkling water to take away. The
barman pulled out a large glass bottle. I had no intention of
carrying that kind of weight with me, so I asked if they had
plastic bottles of water. They did not, but he emptied the
sparkling water into a plastic bottle that he had behind the
counter.

I took my Evian bottle into the bathroom to fill up with
water from the tap and prepared to leave. The air conditioning
was such a welcome relief that I wished I could stay longer, but
I wanted to head back to the trail. I was planning on eating my
packed lunch, so there was no need to linger in the restaurant.
As I left, the barman reminded me that it was necessary to
drink a lot of water in the heat. I agreed, but now that I had
replenished my water supply, I was confident that I was ready
to tackle the rest of my walk.

The Ridgeway continued down the road until it turned off

to the right at the Fox Hill car park. The sign was confusing, and I wasn't sure if I was in the right place or not, so I approached two cyclists in the car park to confirm that the wide trail ahead was indeed the Ridgeway. It was, so I continued on uphill with confidence.

I soon found a small patch of shade alongside the trail and took off my pack, resting it on the ground. I pulled out the bottle of tap water and used it to soak my head, neck, and hair. Instant relief. It was the best thing I had done all day, and in doing so, I learned a new trick to keep cool on hot, sunny walks: keep my hair wet.

I sat down to eat my sandwich and to drink the sparkling water, which was deliciously cold. A man passed in a small car, driving up the Ridgeway byway. After a short rest, during which the sunshine managed to invade my little bit of shade, I stood up and drenched my head once more. The feeling was incredible. I pulled my pack on and continued uphill, feeling refreshed and recharged. It was amazing the difference a little water could make, both inside and out.

The trail climbed Charlbury Hill, a wide, flat track. I passed a barn on the right and continued. Another car passed me slowly and carefully, heading in the opposite direction. Some time on, I passed yet another car, parked alongside the trail. The first car I had seen while eating my lunch was nowhere in sight. I couldn't imagine where all these cars were going. The path was lined, as usual, with fields of grain that had been harvested. Were these people all farmers out inspecting their crops? I doubted it. What were they doing out there?

Random footpaths and bridleways intersected the Ridgeway at intervals. I kept on and was surprised to see, off in the distance, several flags waving. I couldn't see what they were attached to, and I wondered if it were some ice cream stand or coffee shop that wasn't in the guidebook. There certainly seemed to be a lot of activity on this part of the trial. I got excited at the prospect of cold refreshments. The ice-cold water of The Burj had made such a difference in my day that I couldn't begin to imagine how I might feel with a little ice cream. Surely it would be life-changing.

As I approached, I saw it was a large van that someone was living in. There were several flags from different countries (oddly, none of them British nor Irish), waving wildly in the breeze. The van had all sorts of signs on it, and there were an old, rusted outdoor grill and an array of other equipment sitting next to it. Whoever was living there had been installed for some time. It was all so oddly out of place that it had a weird vibe to it, and I hurried onward.

Shortly after, I passed Ridgeway Farm on my left and crossed a quiet country lane to continue ahead. The trail was dotted with trees on either side and beyond the trees were fields of grain. The track was wide, level, and easy to walk on. It was still very sunny, but my head was now cool from the water, so the heat was no longer a problem.

Eventually, the path began to climb once more until it reached a barn with the much-welcomed water tap. I filled up my Evian bottle for my head, then pulled out my water pouch and filled it to the two-liter point. Despite the heat, I had only drunk one liter from my reservoir and the entire 750 ml bottle of sparkling water from The Burj.

I rearranged all my water recipients. Then I crossed yet another quiet country lane to continue onward, the wide track easy to walk along. I became suddenly aware of how tired my feet were, and I realized that I hadn't yet aired them out despite all my stops that day. I found a bit of shade alongside the trail to stop on and pulled off my shoes and socks to cool them off.

It was the hottest day of walking, which meant that it was extra important to keep my feet dry and cool to avoid blisters. I searched in my pack for a pair of fresh socks, and once my feet were dry, I pulled them on. As soon as I put my shoes back on, I could tell I had made the right decision. My feet were notice-ably cooler, drier, and feeling fresh. I knew I was close to my destination for the night in Ashbury, but I didn't want to risk a blister this early on in my journey.

Not long after, the trail came up and out into a clearing. There were a small car park and a sign alongside an inter-secting road. The fingerpost sign indicated that Ashbury was a half-mile down the road to the left. I took the road and headed straight for my B&B. I was tired and looking forward to arriving at my room for a rest. All I wanted was a cup of tea and a shower—the usual.

I walked through the pretty little village, filled with thatched cottages, and in less than fifteen minutes was at my B&B, the Rose & Crown Hotel. I walked straight up to the hotel entrance. It was locked. I walked around to the back entrance until I found a sign indicating that the pub was closed and that guests needed to make a phone call to get access to the rooms outside regular pub hours.

I called, and no one answered. I left a voicemail and waited impatiently. I get ridiculously irritable when I can't check into my room right away after a long walk. It would be one thing if I could get into the pub and have something cold to drink, but at that point, there was no telling when I'd be able to get inside.

There was a shady ledge outside the back door, and I sat down in the shade on the edge of a raised flower bed. After ten minutes of waiting, I retreated to the more comfortable seating in the pub's back garden, which was also shady. Not long after, a cook exited the back door, apologizing and saying that he had just heard my message. He quickly checked me into my room and led me upstairs so I could settle in.

My room was surprisingly huge, with a large bedroom and a smaller dressing room that led to the bathroom, with a large shower. I put some water on for tea and took a cold shower before settling into my room to relax. I saw that I had a missed phone call and voicemail from Court Hill Centre, the hostel I would be staying at the following night. They wanted me to confirm my reservation. I phoned them back and got their voicemail, which had a message proclaiming that they were fully booked and were not accepting reservations. This was not good. I left a message confirming that I would indeed be arriving, but as I was now worried about where I would be staying the following night, I phoned back a few minutes later to speak with a real person and confirm my reservation. Thankfully, all was in order.

After a couple of hours of resting in my room and doing absolutely nothing, I went down for dinner and had a giant salad with salmon, accompanied by a pint of Guinness. After such a long, hot day, all I wanted was something cool and fresh, and the meal was perfect. I ate slowly, watching as the pub filled with diners little by little, and pulled out my iPad mini to type up the day's events for this chapter while they were still fresh in my mind. I slowly drank my pint as I wrote, finally packing up to return to my room once both the chapter and the Guinness were finished.

DAY 3: ASHBURY TO COURT HILL
8.4 MILES (13 KM)

I had a short walk ahead of me on Day 3—just 8.4 miles (13 km.) from Ashbury to Court Hill—but there were several attractions along the way, and I wanted to take my time when visiting them. Awaiting me were Wayland's Smithy (another long barrow), a possible ice cream van in a car park (ice cream was always welcome on a hot day's walk) near Uffington White Horse and Uffington Castle (another hill fort), the Manger (a steep valley below the white horse that was of interest for some reason), Dragon Hill (a chalk hill where St. George supposedly killed the dragon), and Letcombe Castle (yet another hill fort). I woke up at 7:30, had a cup of tea, did my morning meditation exercises, and was ready at 8:30. I went downstairs, where I ordered breakfast and a packed lunch, then ate a leisurely meal before heading back upstairs to pack everything up and get on the trail.

While the weather forecast had predicted rain when I checked it the night before, it now estimated there would be no rain until 3 pm. I hoped to get to my final destination by that hour because I didn't feel like arriving soggy and muddy as I had on my first day in East Kennett. Now that rain was not predicted until mid-afternoon, the earlier part of the day was almost as hot as the day before.

I wet my hair before leaving my room and checking out, hoping to stay cool and refreshed on the trail. I walked back up the road toward the Ridgeway, and the short half-mile to the path felt a bit longer than it had the day before, probably because I was going uphill this time—and on a full stomach. I finally reached the trail, crossing the road to continue on my way toward Court Hill.

As I started down the Ridgeway, a man and his dog got out of a car at the car park located just beside the road. The two of them began walking behind me on the Ridgeway. The trail was a wide, open track flanked on both sides by shrubs and the occasional tree, with golden fields beyond. There was a narrow alternative walkers' path to the right, which I ignored as usual. It had been some time since I had seen a vehicle on the Ridge-way, so I saw no need to leave the little bit of shade I had on the trail and use the sunny footpath instead.

A little while on, I passed a woman walking her dog. The track had narrowed into two small parallel paths, probably made from the tires of vehicles passing down the byway, though the trail was so rustic, I couldn't imagine any car going through here. More trees were lining the Ridgeway now, and I was grateful for the shade and the coolness of the morning.

After just a half-hour on the trail, I reached the sign for Wayland's Smithy and turned off the path to the left. The long barrow was sitting in a clearing under a small group of trees, which kept the entire area shaded. A couple was leaving the site as I entered, and there was no one else inside the area. I had been looking forward to visiting this site ever since I had left the West Kennet Long Barrow, which I had enjoyed so much.

Wayland's Smithy is another Neolithic long barrow and chamber tomb, estimated to have been built starting around

3590 BCE. The site isn't quite as impressive as West Kennet, mainly because there's only one small chamber that you can enter. The site was built in two phases: the first being a timber-chambered barrow, and the second was the stone-chambered one you can enter today. As at West Kennet, large sarsen stones guard the entrance, but the only chamber that you can enter is so small that you can't do more than crawl inside and sit cross-legged, which I did.

I spent about a half-hour at the site, first reading the information board, where I learned the above history of the site. Then I walked all around the barrow, taking photographs. A cyclist rode up into the site, looked around, circled around the barrow's perimeter, then left. It seemed none of the other visitors I witnessed at either of these long barrows had much of an interest in them. I, however, found them particularly fascinating. I loved these ancient sites, and had never seen an area with such a great concentration of them before.

There were offerings here, much like the ones I had seen at West Kennet Long Barrow: an apple sitting on the top of the barrow, some flowers, and a sprig of wheat. I remembered that Lughnasadh, the harvest festival, had occurred earlier in the month, so it was not surprising that these symbols of harvest appeared as offerings here, as they had at West Kennet. I walked up to the top of the barrow and took off my pack and hat, setting them on the ground alongside my poles.

I climbed carefully down into the barrow and saw two small chambers on either side of the entrance, and a shallow chamber at the back, covered by a large sarsen stone. The chambers were all lightly perfumed with incense. I sat down under the large stone and settled in.

It was so much more exposed than the big chamber at West Kennet, making it difficult to settle in and enjoy it. The chambers were open and were visible from the entrance to the site. I closed my eyes and tried to relax. It was hard to get over the awkwardness of someone arriving at the site and seeing me sitting inside. Despite my love for sitting in silence and meditation at these ancient sites, I always feel self-conscious. I'm afraid that people will see me as The Weird Person who meditates in ancient burial chambers—which is ridiculous because anyone who might come across me won't know who I am and will probably never see me again. Though I guess now that you're reading this book, you might come across a random woman meditating in an ancient tomb and wonder if it's me.

I forced myself to sit there a bit longer to enjoy the energy of the place before I climbed out of the barrow. I walked around the site one more time and then left. Part of me wanted to stay there for more time, and another part was uncomfortable with being the weirdo meditating quietly inside the ancient monument. I reminded myself that I could always come back, perhaps on the same trip where I might return to West Kennet.

I clicked on out of the site with my poles and was shortly back on the Ridgeway, which soon crossed a quiet lane to continue toward Uffington Castle, the next attraction on the list. I decided it was time to connect with Richard 4, and I pulled out my phone to record the message of the day, which was "patience with the process."

"Every seed that you sow will grow into that which you want. Bach flowers. PSYCH-K®. Do that work that you need to do to be patient because your impatience may prohibit you from taking the correct actions because you want to rush, rush, rush things that cannot be rushed. Things cannot be rushed. Patience, patience. Patience with the process. Things take time. You're seeing results from the seeds that you are sowing. That woman sent you an email the other day about including you in her article. These things are good. These things come from your visibility. These things come from you putting yourself out there and people seeing you and what you do."

"Patience, patience, patience. Patience with the process"

was another phrase that would become a mantra for my Ridgeway walk. The Richards were also good at giving me catchy phrases to remember their messages. Their words would come to mind at random points on my journey, not only during the week that I walked but afterward in day-to-day life.

A National Trust sign sat to the left of the trail announcing Uffington Castle, and I could see the ridges of the hill fort beyond. I hoped there would be another stile or gate to easily enter the site, and there was, at the top of the hill. I clicked along the smooth chalk trail towards it. There was a cyclist ahead, and I could tell from a distance that he wasn't navigating the path very well. Unlike most of the other cyclists I'd seen on the Ridgeway—who were usually confident—he looked hesitant and fearful.

I glanced away for a moment, and when I looked back up, I saw both him and his cycle laying down on the track. He quickly got back up and seemed to be okay. We greeted each other as we passed, and I acted as though nothing had happened. Only later did I realize that I should have asked if he was okay, though he seemed to be fine. I was so used to having minimal interactions with people on the trail that I had forgotten basic courtesy.

Not long after, I saw the gate to the left with another National Trust sign for Uffington Castle. This ancient site was another early Iron Age hill fort, most likely built in the 7th or 8th century BCE. The fort was much like the others I had already visited on the Ridgeway, except that this one was a much more popular site, as it was located right near the Uffington White Horse. It wasn't the weekend, but it was summer, and there were people everywhere, which was a shock after being mostly alone on the Ridgeway for three days.

I entered the site through the gate, then walked around the trail to the left until I accessed the hill fort on the entrance trail. I climbed up on the ridge to the left and circled clockwise around the inner rim of the hill fort toward the Manger, the White Horse, and Dragon Hill. I could see from above that, despite my guidebook suggesting there might be an ice cream van in the car park during the summer months, it hadn't yet arrived. It was surprising, considering the number of people around, but perhaps at just after 11:00, it was too early. I continued circling until I got a good view of the Manger and Dragon Hill.

The Manger is a strangely shaped, steep valley below the White Horse on the hillside, which is thought to have been formed by ice melting during the last Ice Age. It's quite unlike any other valley I had seen before. Dragon Hill, located just next to the Manger, looks like a miniature Silbury Hill due to its conical shape: unlike Silbury, though, it's a natural chalk hill with an artificially flattened top. Legend has it that this is where St. George killed the dragon and that the bare patch of white chalk where no grass grows is where the dragon's blood supposedly spilled.

I climbed down the hill toward the White Horse, where I could get an even better view of the Manger and Dragon Hill. I stopped to take some photographs; then I sat down to rest without taking off my pack. There were people everywhere: couples and families with children. It looked like I was the only person on my own. It was a fascinating site, but it was overwhelming to see so many people after two days of peace on the remote Ridgeway. There were paragliders too, and one walked up the hill to the right of the White Horse clutching his giant wing and a ton of gear: he had on some enormous suit with this massive thing down his back.

An older couple had approached and sat down near me, on my right. We all watched the paraglider walk past us and then looked at each other, commenting on how much gear he was carrying. It did look excessive, but what did I know—I'd never tried the sport. The woman asked if I were walking the Ridgeway, and after I replied in the affirmative, she asked if I were doing it alone. I said that I was. "Well, you've got pluck," she said in response and wished me luck.

I liked that. Pluck. Feeling plucky, I continued exploring, walking down the hill past the White Horse to get a view of the design. My guidebook had warned that it was difficult to view the horse from on top of the hill, though it was also tricky even if you climbed down the hill to the base. The best views were from the B4507 road, which runs parallel to the Ridgeway in this part, and I was not up for walking that far off the trail.

There are many white horse hill sculptures in Britain, and in fact, there are so many of them in Wiltshire that there is now a 90-mile (145 km) White Horse Trail that visits all of them. The Uffington White Horse in Oxfordshire, however, is the one that inspired them all and was created in 800 BCE. It is such a minimalistic representation of a horse that it could almost be mistaken for some other animal—though which one, I'm not sure. It looks like modern art, but it's almost 3,000 years old.

I climbed back up the hill, then toward the hill fort's inner ridge, where I stopped to read an information sign before circling back to the point where I had first entered it. I climbed down and walked back toward the Ridgeway. Uffington was a beautiful historical area that included four attractions in one, and I felt like I should have stayed longer to explore and rest, but the site was so popular with visitors that I preferred to be on my way. The day was hot and sunny, much like my previous days on the trail, and I wanted to be sure I spaced out my rest stops.

The trail continued downhill, an open white chalk track lined with green grasses on either side and golden fields beyond. There were occasional footpaths and bridleways off to the left and right. Every once in a while, the Ridgeway crossed paths with a quiet country lane. At one point, I saw the road to

Kingston Lisle on the left and completely forgot that it was also the road to Seven Barrows, on the right.

Despite its name, Seven Barrows contains a total of at least 26 barrows, though some sources say there are more than 30 of them in the area, forming a giant Bronze Age cemetery. I had chosen the Ridgeway specifically for its historic sites, and I had been considering making the detour to Seven Barrows. A few minutes after I realized I had passed the turnoff, I checked my guidebook. There was no indication just how far the barrows were located from the Ridgeway, and I wasn't about to risk a long detour. I decided I had seen enough tumuli and that I didn't need to backtrack to visit them. I continued on my journey.

This was a good decision because later investigation on Google Maps once I returned home indicated that the Seven Barrows site was situated a full 2.3 miles (3.7 km) off the Ridgeway. I'm sure it's a fascinating site, but it's probably not worth a 5-mile detour. No wonder my guidebook didn't make more of a fuss about them.

The trail was still wide and chalky, and as it began to head up Kingston Hill, I found a patch of shade on the right-hand side. I took off my pack, wet my head, and sat down for a rest, taking off my shoes and socks. As I did so, I ate the chocolate bar from my very first packed lunch on Day 1. I had been accumulating the uneaten portions of my packed lunches as the days went on. The afternoon was hot, and I wanted to be sure I took it easy, especially since I had plenty of time before I would arrive at my destination that day.

After resting, I continued up Kingston Hill, where the trail grew a bit steep near the top, then walked down the other side toward Down Barn Farm, where I knew I might find a working water tap. Both my guidebook and the book I had read by Andrew Bowden stated that the tap was dry and not working, but when I approached it, I saw that the trough below it was full. I tested the tap, and it worked perfectly. I was thrilled.

I filled both my water bottles and pulled out my water pouch to fill it, too. As usual, I then had to open up my pack and pull a few things out to make it easier to slide the water pouch back down the side. When my backpack was full, it was challenging to fit the full water pouch down the side. I wet my hair once more, and delighting in the coolness of a wet head, I continued down the trail.

I saw a truck with men unloading some equipment up ahead along the left side of the trail. I greeted them as I passed; they ignored me completely, which seemed odd considering that I must have been the first person to walk past them in a while The trail was wide and chalky, with a secondary path that ran alongside it to the right, made of dirt and grass. I walked along that little path until I saw a horse and its rider coming toward me; I returned to the main chalky trail to give the horse more room. I am always a bit wary of walking alongside horses —I never know how they might react.

The Ridgeway shortly came out onto a road, where it turned right, and then crossed the street to head back into its usual natural setting. I passed a field on the left that bore signs warning of low flying model aircraft, and I saw a man carrying a small model airplane in his hands as he crossed the field. Two cars were parked there, presumably more model plane enthusiasts.

The trail was wide and chalky, deeply rutted from vehicles that had passed through over the years. I crossed paths with a couple heading in the opposite direction, the first people I had seen in some time. I walked on in the scorching heat until I saw a shady patch under a tree and headed over for another rest, sitting down on the grassy bank to eat my lunch.

As I ate, a car suddenly came down the byway in front of me. Its occupants looked as surprised to see me as I was to see them, much like the farmer who had passed me on his tractor the previous day near Liddington Castle. They passed just inches from where I was sitting and continued on their way, slowly navigating the very rustic byway. Not long after, I saw a walker, laden with a huge pack, with a rolled-up camping mat strapped to the bottom of his pack. A camper, the first I'd seen on the trail. Unlike the South Downs Way, the Ridgeway has numerous places to camp along the route, making it a much better choice for people wanting to camp. I greeted him, and he also looked shocked to see me apologizing and explaining that he had been lost in thought. I knew the feeling. It was hard to be social after so much solitude.

Not long after the camper continued on his way, I prepared my things to get back on the trail myself. I knew I was close to my final destination that day, and I could take it easy on the remaining portion of my walk. It felt just as hot as it had the day before, and there were still no rain clouds in sight, despite the forecast that morning. I soon passed the camper I had seen on my break, eating his lunch in a patch of shade to the left of the trail. I greeted him again as I continued on past.

The trail led straight on, passing a quiet lane where I stopped to let a massive tractor pass by—the first farm machinery I had seen on the actual trail. The Ridgeway eventually opened up once more into two paths, the sunny main byway with a shady, tree-lined footpath to the left. I opted for the footpath this time since the main byway was open, hot, and sunny, and I had had enough of the sun that day. It soon became apparent that no one had maintained the footpath in some time. It was narrow and overgrown, and I eventually reached a point where I could continue no longer. I backtracked to a place where I remembered seeing an opening in the brush, and there I pushed through to the primary, sunny trail.

I saw trails off to the left for Letcombe Bassett, a small

village just a half-mile (one km) off the path, ignoring them. I knew I was getting closer to that afternoon's destination, and I was looking forward to it, though I also knew it had been a short walk that day. It was too hot to be out walking, even though I continued to wet my hair regularly with my water bottle. The track was much wider now and looked like it had recently been coated with a dusting of chalk. It glowed bright white in the hot sun as I walked, amplifying its effect.

I passed another country lane and kept going. I could see Segsbury Camp, also known as Letcombe Castle, off to the left. I had planned on visiting it, and I pulled out my guidebook to see how to get there. It turned out that the only route was via the lane I had just passed, and I didn't feel like backtracking to visit the hill fort, which was the fourth one I had encountered on my Ridgeway walk thus far.

I debated what to do: on the one hand, I wanted to take in all the archaeological sites that the Ridgeway had to offer, but on the other hand, I was hot and tired and wanted to reach my destination that evening. I eventually chose to keep going, bypassing Letcombe Castle. I was disappointed to miss the site, but I had already seen three hill forts this week and one earlier that same day.

Letcombe Castle is yet another Iron Age hill fort, and at 30 acres in size, it is double the size of Barbury Castle. The site is so large that it's dissected by a road, much like the Avebury stone circle. According to my guidebook, it's a much less popular site than Barbury, and visitors will often find themselves alone to explore. It also has the added benefit of being located just about 100 yards/meters off the Ridgeway, making it easily accessible for walkers—if you catch the turnoff.

The blindingly bright white chalk byway continued for some time, making me wish I carried sunglasses with me on my walks. I never did—England wasn't sunny enough for that! (Or was it?) There were some trees and shrubs along the trail, but they did nothing to provide shade. I had only walked about eight miles that day, but it felt like more. I passed some red brick cottages to my left and arrived at the A338 road, my turnoff to Court Hill.

I turned left down the road and somehow managed to miss the turnoff to Court Hill Centre, where I would be staying, despite some rather large and obvious signs advertising the Court Hill tea room. I walked a fair way down the road, which sloped downhill, before realizing something was wrong. I pulled out my phone, which luckily had a signal, and checked Google Maps to discover that I had indeed made the dreaded mistake of walking past the turnoff, and I had to turn around and go back up the hill toward my accommodation for that evening.

About ten minutes later, I arrived at Court Hill Centre, where I discovered that I was only one of two people staying that night, despite their voicemail message proclaiming that they were full for the night. All my worries evaporated in one second. I had been concerned all day about being over-whelmed by a hostel full of people after three days of solitude on the Ridgeway, and I had worried for nothing.

I was delighted to have the room to myself; the last time I had stayed at a youth hostel was twenty years earlier in 1996, and I hadn't been looking forward to sharing the room with three other people. I'm an introvert, and after being all alone on a trail for hours on end, I feel even less social, so you can imagine how unpalatable the prospect of sharing a room was to me.

You might wonder why I even risked booking a bed there. I had booked at Court Hill for a couple of reasons: it was the closest place to stay near the Ridgeway, and I had wanted to give hosteling a try. I still planned to walk the Camino de Santiago one day, and the most common way to do that was to stay in group accommodation rather than private rooms or

B&Bs, as I was used to in England. The relief I felt upon discovering that the hostel was empty and that I would have a room of my own reminded me of everything I needed to know about myself: I'm a solo walker. I enjoy my peace and solitude, and I'm not keen on sharing a room with a stranger after a long day on the trail. My Court Hill experiment had served me well, because I realized how little I wanted to share a room with other people. I resolved to avoid hostels in the future whenever possible.

I unpacked my things and headed straight for the tiny shower to cool off after my hot walk. Then, I went to the tea room for a cup of tea and a cold bottle of sparkling water. To me, there's nothing like sparkling water for quenching my thirst. However, the tea room closed shortly after that, so I took my water bottle to the courtyard to relax in the shade as I typed up this day's chapter. As I wrote, I watched out of the corner of my eye as George, the lone guinea fowl, wandered around the grassy area. Eventually, it started to rain a bit, and I headed back inside.

I was a bit apprehensive about having dinner with the other guests at the Court Hill Centre. I'm terrible at small talk, but I had forgotten how easy it is to speak with other walkers. We have one very obvious topic of conversation at hand: the trail we are on. We talked about the trails we'd already walked and about other routes we wanted to do in the future. And that's what the dinner conversation was like with the one other guest, who turned out to be the same person I'd crossed paths with on the trail earlier when I was resting in the shade. He was camping at Court Hill and pitched his tent outside the dorms, on a grassy area.

We discussed the trail we had traversed thus far, the weird van with the flags we had both seen, where we had stayed on previous nights, and the history of the Ridgeway. He was a history teacher, though unfortunately, he didn't specialize in the era in which most of the Ridgeway's sites had been built. We talked about Uffington and the legend of St. George and the dragon. I learned that, despite being the patron saint of England, St. George had never set foot in the country. So much for the Uffington legend, though it did make the strange, flat-topped hill seem a bit more interesting.

After dinner, I retired straight to my room. I climbed up into one of the top bunks and settled in to read before sleeping. Court Hill was quiet and peaceful, perfect for a good rest after a hot day's walk. The tranquil, remote feeling of the place was the ideal complement to the Ridgeway's quiet peace. I love bunk beds and was thrilled at the prospect of sleeping in the top bunk in a room that I had all to myself. Eventually, I grew tired and turned out the light, falling asleep quickly.

DAY 4: COURT HILL TO GORING
14.8 MILES (23.5 KM)

The following morning, it appeared there was a third guest at Court Hill, and we all three had breakfast together. The third guest was not a walker but was driving down to the New Forest and had stopped at Court Hill along the way. I discussed the dismal outlook for the day ahead with the other Ridgeway walker. We were both traveling with the same Trailblazer guide, and it looked like yet another day of flat, wide, open byways with views of farmland—yet this time, there would be no ancient historical attractions to spice things up. It sounded like a day of tedious walking, and that's what it ended up being. The other walker planned to speed-walk his way through it, and I planned to do the exact opposite: take as many breaks as possible, hopefully making the journey more comfortable. It was a much longer day than previous ones had been.

It was a glorious overcast, cloudy, misty morning, and we were both eager to get on the trail before the sun broke through the gray. I had never been so excited to see cloud cover. The other walker departed just minutes before I did, and I saw him ahead on the main road as we returned to the Ridgeway. I stopped to take a photograph of the misty fields across the street, and when I looked back, I could no longer see him. Within minutes, I was back on the Ridgeway myself, and I never saw him the entire day—or ever again, for that matter. He was only walking the western half of the trail, and this would be his last day. He had speed-walked off into the mists.

There were no water taps on this stage of the Ridgeway, so I had left Court Hill prepared with all of my water recipients filled to the brim: my water pouch, my Evian bottle, and my half-liter of water for splashing on my head. It was a cloudy morning, but the sun was sure to break through at some point, so I wanted to be sure I had more than enough water. I carried a total of four liters (almost a gallon) between my pouch and my bottles. That meant four kilos, or nearly nine pounds, of weight in water. A heavy pack indeed.

The Ridgeway passed some old farm buildings to the left, went under some trees, and then resumed the landscape that was so typical of the western half of the trail: wide, open chalky track, with fields beyond. In less than a half-hour, I crossed the B4494 road, where two women were getting their horses ready for a ride to the right-hand side of the trail.

I paused. The wide track continued to the left. To the right, there was a familiar Ridgeway information board alongside a much smaller trail. I looked back and forth between the two, wondering which path I needed to take, and one of the women said, "If you're looking for the Ridgeway, it's the one to the right." I thanked her and continued. I soon passed a large marble monument to my right. I climbed up it, walked all around it, and then hopped back down to remain on the trail.

From there, the Ridgeway got a little tricky. Several different trails headed more or less in the same direction, and the signs were not always clear as to which one was the actual Ridgeway. It became a matter of simply choosing one trail and keeping an eye on where all the others led. The tracks ran all across

Ridgeway Down, Ardington Down, and East Ginge Down. It was easy walking along the chalky, grassy path. There were no farm vehicles in sight, and nor was there anyone else visible on the trail.

I stopped in some shade on the left side of the trail for a rest. I needed a way to break up the track's monotony, and I still resolved to take as many rest stops as I felt like taking. I had left just after 9 am, and I had plenty of time to reach Goring, despite this day's walk being my longest thus far.

I spotted the dark figure of a man off in the distance, and I thought he might have been the walker from Court Hill. I soon realized that he had a dog with him, so it must be someone else. I walked over Cuckhamsley Hill and on toward Bury Down, the scenery remaining the same. My guidebook directed walkers to "continue the easy walking on this seemingly never-ending broad, grassy track." This instruction seemed to apply to the entire day's walk, save the end, as I approached the twin villages of Streatley and Goring.

Eventually, I caught up to the man and his dog, then passed them just before I reached Bury Down. I crossed a road and continued, stopping for a second break in the shade on the right-hand side of the vast, open trail. The day was still overcast, but it was getting warmer. I pulled out a bag of crisps and ate it, craving the salt. It had been an hour since my previous rest stop, and it seemed like not much had happened since then. The monotonous scenery made this a very uneventful portion of the trail. How had I tired of the beautiful Ridgeway so soon? It must be the heat.

I got up and continued on my way, and before long, the trail sloped downhill before it passed under the A34 road. Here, the path suddenly became lush and green, filled with leafy trees, a delightful contrast to the rest of the trail. It was like an underpass oasis. The Ridgeway came back up on the other side of the A34 and promptly resumed its usual landscape, the open track running straight on between fields. I stopped to read a memorial stone off to the left, which marked the death of a young soldier, Hugh Frederick Grosvenor, who was killed on that spot in an armored car accident in 1947 at the age of 19.

The Ridgeway continued straight ahead. I was aware that there was an old water tap that had been capped as of the time of research of my guidebook, and I was curious to see if it was now working. I walked up to it, discovered that it was still capped, then I continued. Thankfully, I had more than enough water for the day, and I certainly didn't need to add weight to my pack by filling up my bottles.

I thought of the Richards and my previous days of channeling. They were sure to break up the monotonousness of the trail, but this was meant to be my rest day. The Richards were very clear: the first four days were for channeling each one of them, this was to be a rest day, and then I would resume connecting with them for the final four days of my journey. The instructions had made sense when they had given them to me, but now I missed the channeling, which would have brought some entertainment to the trail's tediousness. Perhaps they had planned it that way: I needed to be alone with my thoughts on this day.

Not long after the capped water tap, the trail turned left. I passed a family of cyclists, and I stopped to pull out my sun hat, which I had left in my pack thanks to the morning's cool mist. It was getting hotter and brighter, and I had reached the point where I needed to cover my head. Despite the cooler day, I was regularly dousing my head with water at each break and sometimes in between rest stops. Wetting my head seemed to be the answer to all my problems on this trail—except for the monotony of this day. Perhaps if I had discovered this trick on my South Downs walk, it would have made things easier for me.

After I passed a dismantled rail line, I stopped along the left side of the trail for yet another rest. It had been a little over an hour since my previous stop, and nothing much had happened since then. The path had been more of the same. I drank one of my juice boxes, and took off my shoes and socks to air out my feet as I rested. When I was ready, I put my shoes and socks back on and continued on my journey.

The trail went steadily up a little hill, crossing a few other paths in the process, and finally changed scenery, now running between shady trees. The map indicated I was approaching Streatley Warren, where walkers might see many rabbits around the track. Given the monotony of the day, I was looking forward to some rabbit spotting. They might very well prove to be the highlight of the day. Sadly, I only saw one rabbit, lying dead under an old tire to the right of the path. Not what I was hoping for. I forged onward.

The Ridgeway finally changed its landscape, gradually becoming lush. Its shady byway ran between an increasing amount of green leafy trees until it descended steadily downward to come out on a road, where I stepped aside to let a small tractor pass. At this point, the Ridgeway entered some bustling civilization. It was every bit as jarring as the busy road near the Burj on Day 2: after hours of the quiet, remote trail, I was once again walking down a paved street with cars noisily passing by. Was I approaching my final destination for that day?

The Ridgeway continued straight down the road, which was now lined with cottages on the right-hand side. I hadn't yet eaten my sandwich, and I was suddenly hungry. I desperately looked for a place to stop and eat. I saw the first bench of the day by the side of the road: two logs with a board nailed across the top. It wasn't the idyllic lunch stop I had become used to, but it was good enough. I pulled out my sandwich and ate half of it. It was made of lettuce, tomato, and cheese and had survived the journey remarkably well.

I had just 40 minutes to go on the trail, and I was anxious to arrive at my B&B, so I didn't linger. After eating, I resumed walking, clicking with my poles along the side of the road. I passed several cottages, then a golf club. Finally, I approached the busy A417 road, where the Ridgeway turns right, continuing down the sidewalk. It was a bit overwhelming, all the noise of civilization. Cars were rushing by as I walked quickly through Streatley on my way to Goring, which was just across the river.

And then I saw it: the Thames! After days of long, hot fields, it was a beautiful, refreshing sight. The river was lined with restaurants and cafes, and there were boats moored up alongside the banks. Several boats were arranging themselves within Goring Lock, waiting for the last one to get in before they could let the water out and get down to the lower level of the river.

I stood there a moment, enjoying the lushness of the river before I continued onward. It was such a contrast to everything I had seen thus far on the Ridgeway, and it was a clear sign I was entering the eastern stage of the trail. As I approached Goring, the village that sits on the opposite side of the Thames from Streatley, I pulled out my phone to navigate to Melrose Cottage, the B&B I had booked for the evening. It was a pleasant 15-minute walk through the village to get to my accommodation, and I was so looking forward to showering and resting in my room.

Unfortunately, no one was around when I arrived. I rang the doorbell. Nothing. I knocked on the door. Nothing. I phoned the B&B and left a message on the voicemail. I called the B&B's mobile number and left another voicemail. I was hot, tired, and frustrated. I just wanted my room, a shower, and a cup of tea. And I was getting grumpy, as I'm sure you can tell.

As I waited for the B&B owner to arrive, it started to rain, so I huddled under the small overhang outside the door and considered my options. I hadn't yet paid for my accommodation, so perhaps I could find somewhere else to stay. I started phoning around and found a much more expensive option in a pub in the village center. As it was readily accessible, it was an appealing alternative. As I debated what to do, the B&B owner pulled up in her car, surprised to see me so early.

Despite being so annoyed at having to wait, I forced myself to put on my happy face and greet the B&B owner. There was no sense in being unpleasant, and I knew I was not good at dealing well with surprises, such as having to wait to get into my accommodation at the end of a long walk. That was my own problem, and I knew it.

She was very friendly and showed me upstairs to my room and the bathroom, shared with the other guests. I showered, then went back to my room and washed my clothes in the sink inside my bedroom, hanging my pants on the pedestal fan that cooled off the room. Because my summer walking trousers were light and fast-drying, the fan would prove as useful as the heated towel rack had in drying them overnight. I opened the window to let the fresh air in, as the room was a bit warm, and I relaxed with a cup of tea on my bed. Dinner would mean a 10-15 minute walk back into the village, and I wasn't quite ready for that yet. I settled in for a rest.

Even though I hadn't planned on responding to emails while I was away, I quickly checked on my phone and saw a new message from a potential client. I decided to give him a quick phone call as I relaxed in my room and instantly regretted the decision. The call got me out of relaxation mode and into work mode. The man was difficult and negative. After a half-hour of listening to his philosophies of life, I insisted that he needed to figure out precisely what he wanted to work on and told him that I would send him a questionnaire that I use as an intake form. Whether or not he ended up working with me, I told him, filling it out would help him get clarity. Getting off the call, I emailed the form to him using my phone. Not surprisingly, I never heard from him again.

I resolved not to revisit my emails for the rest of the week, disappointed with myself for caving in and checking my phone. I realized it was time for dinner, and after reading through the information packet in my room, I decided I would head into the village for a curry. It had been a long, hot journey, but I felt the need for a very substantial meal for some reason. I slowly made my way downstairs and into the village, where I was the first to arrive at the Indian restaurant. I would be having a very early dinner that evening.

After finishing off a plate of creamy chicken korma and a plain lassi (I was clearly in the mood for comfort food after such a tedious walk), I began the slow journey back to my B&B, legs, and feet aching. The restaurant was filling up, and I decided to record the day's events—or, rather, the uneventful details of that day on the trail—on my iPad back in my room. Today had been my longest day's walk, and it would make for my shortest chapter of the book thus far. I felt guilty for disliking this portion of the trail. The Ridgeway had been so magical and beautiful for the first three days. It almost felt like I was unfaithful to it by criticizing this fourth day of walking.

DAY 5: GORING TO WATLINGTON
14.7 MILES (23.5 KM)

After the previous day's walk, I was so tired that I had the best night's sleep thus far on the Ridgeway. It was a warm night, and I left the window open and slept with the ceiling fan running. I woke up just once to cover up with the duvet before dawn when the night finally began to cool off. When the alarm sounded, I felt fantastic. I was fully recovered after my long day of walking, and I was ready for another long day on the trail.

It was supposed to be cooler than on previous days, yet sunny all day long. I filled up my water pouch, and my two bottles, then I headed down for breakfast, where I shared a table with two other lodgers, who were regular guests working in the area on a long project. After a simple cooked breakfast (I was beginning to tire of such heavy morning meals), I was ready to get on the trail by 8:30. It was good that I had an early start, because I would somehow manage to take eight full hours to complete my day's journey, not arriving at my accommodation in Watlington until 4:30 pm.

I quickly walked from my B&B back to the Ridgeway. It seemed much faster now that I knew where I was going. When

I reviewed my notes for this book, however, I realized that I could have continued walking along the Ridgeway the afternoon before, approaching my B&B from the other side, which would have made my return to the trail much quicker and easier. Unfortunately, I had no idea at the time, and I retraced my steps the way I had come the day before. I made a mental note for myself, should I ever return to this trail.

The morning was pleasantly cool and refreshing, and the first part of the walk went along the Thames, which helped keep the trail cool. The Ridgeway wound through a small residential neighborhood before returning alongside the river, with the Thames to the trail's left. The path was situated up above the river, shaded by leafy green trees. It was a pleasant contrast to my previous days on the Ridgeway. It was clear that I had entered the eastern half of the trail, known for being more shaded and protected than the western half. As I walked, I passed one walker out for a stroll, and one runner. It was a quiet morning in Goring, except for the trains that frequently ran down the tracks, which sat to the right of the trail, beyond the houses that lined the Ridgeway.

I followed the path out of Goring, on through an open field, and into the tiny village of South Stoke. I passed the St. Andrews church on my right but walked right on past. I had seen so many churches that week, and I wasn't yet in need of a rest. I planned to keep going for the first part of the morning to take advantage of the cooler weather.

Once I was out of South Stoke, the Ridgeway snaked over to run right alongside the Thames. Motorboats hummed along the river in both directions. It was a beautiful sunny day, and people were out on the water. Surprisingly, there were very few people on the trail now that I had left Goring and South Stoke: I passed only one man walking his dog, just as I approached the double-arched viaducts that carried the trains over the river.

The Ridgeway continued alongside the river for some time. A woman passed in a motorboat, looked over at me, and waved. I lifted a Pacerpole in response and waved it back at her. Shortly after, the trail veered off to the right, away from the Thames, and that was the last I saw of the river that day. It had been such a welcome change from the dry, open trail of the previous days, but it had marked a change in scenery along the Ridgeway, dividing it into two very different segments: dry, open farmland in the west and lush, shady woods in the east.

Not long after, the trail passed through the churchyard of the 14th century Church of St. Mary in North Stoke. I wandered in and left a pound coin in its collection slot, as I usually did when visiting churches on my walks. I took a couple of photographs, then walked back out into the churchyard, searching for a shaded bench, which I spotted near the exit gate. I took off my pack and sat down to rest and review my guidebook.

It was a quick break, and I was soon back on my way as the Ridgeway headed straight through a golf course and down a tree-lined path that protected walkers (or so I hoped) from stray golf balls. I was always nervous about walking through a golf course, fearful of getting hit with a stray ball. I hurried to get through it as quickly as possible. The trail was flat here and continued straight out of the golf course and on ahead until it abruptly turned right before the A4130 road.

Here, the trail followed parallel to the noisy road as it continued straight on under shady trees, down a dirt path. Eventually, it came out onto another busy road that I had to cross to continue down the Ridgeway. At this point, the trail ran alongside Grim's Ditch, which, according to my guidebook, was built during the Iron Age as a land boundary. The path went along a short ridge, up above the farmland that extended down both sides of the trail. The Ridgeway was lined by trees and was a narrow but easy footpath to follow. It was a nice change from the wide byways of previous days.

The Ridgeway continued alongside Grim's Ditch, running straight past one quiet country lane, then another, then down the side of an open field before heading up into Oaken Copse. I sat down on a small log to the left of the trail, taking off my pack and setting it down beside me. I aired out my feet, which were already getting hot.

For the first time that week, I hadn't purchased a lunch that morning from my B&B. I had so many elements left over from previous lunches that I had enough to piece together a full meal. I ate the second half of my lettuce, tomato, and cheese sandwich from Court Hill, which I had stored overnight in the mini-fridge of my room at Melrose Cottage. I opened a bag of crisps and ate them, and finished the meal off with an apple.

After a long rest, I pulled on fresh socks before putting my shoes back on. A lone walker approached from a distance, greeted me, and continued in the same direction as I was headed. He was the first person I had seen in over an hour. After it had departed from the riverbank, the trail had grown quiet, with the same remote feeling of the previous days on the Ridgeway. I slowly pulled my pack on and got ready to leave, allowing time for the walker to advance before me, so I wasn't walking right behind him. It was the last I saw of him.

The trail seemed to have lost Grim's Ditch, as it wasn't very apparent from the main path, but soon it became clear that it was still present: as the Ridgeway wound gently uphill, a great ditch could be seen directly to the left of the path, with another ridge on the other side. It continued this way for some time, the trail crossing over to the other side of the ditch at one point and then going straight down the middle.

Sooner than I expected it, the Ridgeway came up and out of Grim's Ditch, and I saw a sign for the first water tap on the trail that day. I refilled my bottles, then my water pouch. I doused my head before heading back on my way along the path, which was now following the left-hand side of the ditch.

It crossed to the other side for one last time before the ditch was over, and the Ridgeway turned left toward Nuffield. The trail passed through a field alongside rolls of harvested wheat before coming out onto a road and turning right. Immediately beyond was the Holy Trinity Church, where I planned to rest again. It had been over an hour since my lunch break, and I still intended to take many rest stops, as this was my second long day in a row.

There had once been a pub in this little village, but it had closed years before. Even my guidebook, which was four years old, stated that it was closed at the time of research in 2011. In response to the pub's closing, some genius at the church came up with the idea of providing a rest stop for walkers: a sign at the gate to the churchyard proclaimed that there was self-serve tea and cake inside.

I wandered in and quickly spotted the tea station to the left. I pulled off my pack and set down my poles. There was a Brita water filter jug, a kettle, a tray with tea, instant coffee, sugar, and a mini-fridge with milk and fresh home-made fruitcake. I put the kettle on for a cup of tea and took a piece of cake from the fridge. I popped a more generous than usual donation into the church box and then sat down and ate the cake as I waited for the kettle to boil.

It was cool and quiet inside. I finished the cake, then realized that I should air out my feet once more. The church was probably not the best place to do that, so I gathered up my things and brought my cup of tea out to the shaded bench in the churchyard to cool off my feet.

It was a hot day. I wasn't suffering the heat as much as I had in the early days of my walk, but my feet felt it. After allowing them to dry, I checked to see if my first socks had dried from the heat so I could put them back on. They had, and I was thankful for the fresh, cool socks.

After a much longer break than I had anticipated, I popped back into the church to throw away my disposable cup, then headed around the back of the churchyard to use their portable toilet, which was surprisingly clean and pleasant. I crossed the street and headed down the Ridgeway through my second golf course of the day. According to my calculations, I still had three hours left to go on the trail, which seemed impossible since I had set out early that morning. My rest stops had been many and long that day.

This time, however, the Ridgeway went straight across the fairways. There were strategically placed signposts throughout, which I had to squint to see across the golf course. Fortunately, there were few people out golfing, and I didn't have to dodge any wayward balls. Still, I was relieved once I was finally out of the golf course, and I passed two houses. The trail went right past their front doors and down their driveways before crossing a road and passing into a small wooded area.

From here, the Ridgeway went through a large open field, and I was briefly out in the sun once more, a reminder of my early days on the western half of the trail. I passed another small wooded area and then a second wide, open field. I passed through Ewelme Park, thought to have been established in the late 14th century and once a royal deer park.

I continued, passing some barns before turning right and heading down a fairly steep dirt path, where I came out on a quiet lane, with St. Botolph's church to my right. A couple was approaching the churchyard from the opposite direction. We greeted each other, and I entered the gate first, eyes darting around to find the first shaded bench for a rest. I saw a partially shaded one to the church's left and walked all around it until I finally determined that this was indeed the best bench for a rest—it was blessed with the best shade. I promptly installed myself on it and performed my usual shoe and sock ritual.

It had been exactly an hour since I had left the church in Nuffield, and the time had passed quickly. I sat and rested for some time until I saw the couple leave the churchyard. I pulled on fresh socks and went around to view the church, which was gorgeous from the inside.

The original St. Botolph's parish church of Swyncombe, a Grade II listed building, was early Norman but had been heavily restored in 1850 and again in the 20th century. The church is most famous for the carpet of snowdrops that bloom in the churchyard every February. Despite its remote location, the church is so well known for its abundance of flowers that there have been reported cases of snowdrop theft, which is certainly not something you encounter every day.

From there, I walked down the lane, then crossed another quiet country road. The Ridgeway went down a hill, through a field, and back up the other side before entering the woods. I was tired, and my feet were aching. It was clear that they had a limit to just how much walking they were willing to tolerate each day in the heat. Not only does the weight of a big back-pack add stress to my feet, but the long hours of walking tends to make them swell within my shoes.

It was time to reconnect with Richard 1. So I got into channeling mode, pulling out my phone to begin recording the message: "You would benefit from a morning ritual. You would benefit from reading the Hal Elrod book [The Miracle Morning: The 6 Habits That Will Transform Your Life Before 8 am]. Not just the writing book [I had recently read The Miracle Morning for Writers: How to Build a Writing Ritual That Increases Your Impact and Your Income (Before 8 am)], but the original book. You will want to adapt this ritual for your needs. You will not want to use it as it is exactly prescribed in the book. You will want to make your own version."

After reading *The Miracle Morning for Writers*, I had been excited to create my version of a morning ritual but hadn't bothered to do much about it. I felt that reading the original book behind the Miracle Morning concept would be the motivation that I needed to create a morning practice that worked for me. And according to Richard 1, this routine would give me peace of mind, which was the message he had given me on my circular Avebury walk.

I was carefully following the handwritten maps in my Trailblazer guidebook, tracking my location. I saw that I had just one and a half maps' worth of walking to go before reaching Watlington, my final destination for that day. Because this was the second time I had hiked a National Trail using these maps, I had grown used to measuring my walk in terms of how many pages of maps I had left, although sometimes I calculated my journey in terms of distance or time. On the shorter days, calculating distance traveled and distance to my evening's destination wasn't so important. Still, by mentally splitting the path into portions, it was easier to get through the longer, more challenging days on the trail.

The Ridgeway was now a narrow path that ran down the edge of a field lightly shaded by trees to the trail's right side. There were blackberries, too, and I stopped at one point to pick and eat some. I was anxious to be done with my walk for the day, but I had eaten an early lunch and was getting a little hungry again. My stomach seemed to have forgotten the tea and cake I had eaten at the church.

The trail came out alongside a farm, where it turned right, once again down a wide byway that was so reminiscent of previous days on the Ridgeway. I crossed a quiet country lane, then another off to the left. At this point, I knew I was close to the turnoff for Watlington. I was distracted by a local walker, who suggested I take a permissive footpath that ran through fields to the right of the Ridgeway. I was hesitant to do so because I didn't want to miss my turnoff to Watlington, and I couldn't see any benefit to walking the parallel trail.

Upon hearing where I was headed, he suggested I take a different shortcut through a field on the left. I was reluctant to do that, too, as I didn't want to get lost. I had seen in my guidebook that there were two main roads into Watlington, and I planned to take the second one as it ran straight into the village, very near my accommodation for that evening. I didn't want to risk getting the roads mixed up.

I ignored his advice and kept on, down the wide track, which turned into a paved road. I kept straight, then turned left at the first main crossroad, which unfortunately was the road I had planned not to go down. It was much busier than I had expected, and I kept having to cross from one side to the other, walking along whichever side had the flattest verge to walk on. It reminded me a bit of my first stressful afternoon on the South Downs Way when I had to walk two miles off the trail to reach my accommodation for that night.

Because I hadn't walked down the right road, I was confused when I arrived in the village and had to pull out my guidebook and check the map to find out where I was. There was no mobile signal in the village, so I couldn't use Google Maps to help me navigate, as I had been doing to find my way through the villages each afternoon to my B&B. Using my guidebook, I estimated how to get to the Fat Fox Inn from where I was, and I headed straight to it. I was hot, tired, and aching, and as usual, all I wanted was a cup of tea and a shower. My desires were so predictable at the end of a long walk.

I entered the pub and walked straight up to the bar to ask about my room. Fortunately, this time I would not have to wait to check in! I was led out the pub's back door, past a barbecue grill that was being prepared for that evening's dinner, and to my room, which was small and strangely shaped, with two twin beds. None of the walls seemed to come together in right angles; they were all askew. It was an old building.

I peeled off my sticky, sweaty clothes, hopped in the shower, then put the kettle on for a cup of tea as I began washing my clothes in the sink. I was thrilled to see that my room at the Fat Fox had a heated towel rack. As I waited for dinnertime at the pub, I browsed through my guidebook to see what awaited me the next day. I soon discovered that the Chinnor & Princes Risborough Railway ran historical steam trains through Chinnor station, located just a short walk off the Ridgeway. Formerly known as the Watlington and Princes Risborough Railway Company, the line first opened in 1872 and later closed to passenger traffic in 1957 and to goods and parcel traffic in 1961.

After the line's closure, the section from Chinnor to Watlington was closed completely, and the track was lifted. However, the following section from Chinnor to Princes Risborough was retained to serve the local cement works in Chinnor. Eventually, this too was closed in 1989 and remained as such until 1994, when the first passenger service since 1957 began running return trips to Wainhill Halt. This route was later extended to Thame Junction, and today it continues to Princes Risborough. There is no platform for passengers to disembark however, there were plans to open one soon after.

I love trains, especially older trains, and I've been fascinated with the old, closed railways ever since I first walked the Downs Link, which followed an old rail line. I began to investigate online on my phone, and I discovered the next day's timetable on the Chinnor & Princes Risborough Railway website. It was a Saturday, so there were short 12-minute rides to Wainhill and back, and longer ones continued to Princes Risborough along the Risborough Preview route, making for almost an hour's journey.

I planned to arrive in time for the 11:30 Risborough Preview train, which would take me to that day's walking destination and back. The scheduled train for that day was unfortunately not a steam train, but rather an old electric one called Linda the Lymington Flyer, which was the only surviving refurbished 3 CEP, 1198 (whatever that is), and one of only three complete train units of its type left in the world. Linda was first built in 1960 and was later refurbished in 1983.

I was convinced that this was a necessary detour for me to take from the Ridgeway, and I calculated how long it would take me to reasonably walk from Watlington to Chinnor station. It appeared doable, depending on how early I started the following morning. By the time I was ready to head back to the pub for dinner, I was thoroughly excited about my detour to the Chinnor & Princes Risborough Railway the following morning. While not exactly an ancient site, it would still make for a fascinating historical side trip.

It was a Friday night, and the pub filled up quickly. I settled into a quiet table near the back and ordered my meal, pulling out my iPad to record the day's journey as I waited. Eventually, there were so many people that it was a bit overwhelming, and I retreated to my room to finish typing up the day's walk.

DAY 6: WATLINGTON TO PRINCES RISBOROUGH

11 MILES (18 KM)

I was anxious to get on the trail by 8:30 at the latest since I wanted to reach Chinnor early enough to catch the heritage train to Princes Risborough at 11:30. I had booked breakfast for eight, but it was slow in coming, and the sandwich I had ordered for the trail was even slower in the making. I ate quickly once my food arrived. Then, I returned to my room to put my things together after breakfast. I checked out of the hotel and waited a few minutes longer for my BLT sandwich to be ready. The Fat Fox was the first place I had stayed along the Ridgeway that didn't offer a full packed lunch for walkers, but rather just a sandwich—for the same price as a full lunch had cost on the previous days. It seemed that the name of the inn hinted at how little food the fox had left for the rest of us.

It was clear that I had left the world of B&Bs that catered to walkers and entered the real world once again. The eastern half of the Ridgeway was much more urban, with larger villages. Everything had a different feel here. It was like the magic of the western half of the Ridgeway had dissipated a little.

It was 8:45 by the time I was able to leave the Fat Fox, and I was concerned about arriving in Chinnor with enough time to catch the train. I had decided to return via Hill Road, the more direct route back to the Ridgeway, though it would mean bypassing a short section of the trail between the street I took the previous day and Hill Road. I tend to be a bit of a purist: I don't like skipping portions of a trail. At the same time, I couldn't bear the thought of facing that busy road once again, and I wanted to get going to catch the train at Chinnor. I knew the timing was tight.

Hill Road was fantastic: this was the road I had initially wanted to walk down to access Watlington on the previous day, and the street was quiet and peaceful, with a paved sidewalk up to the Ridgeway. It was the perfect access road between the trail and the village.

Few people were out on this Saturday morning. As I crossed the street to start on the trail, I saw a couple walking with a dog behind me. I was disappointed to be starting the path so close to other people because I loved being alone out on the trail—as you might have already gathered. However, they ambled along slowly, and I soon lost them behind me, never to be seen again.

The Ridgeway headed straight down a path bordered by trees on both sides, and I was able to walk quickly, faster than on previous days. The morning was chilly, and it drizzled a bit at the start of my walk. It was pleasant and refreshing. The path was easy going and climbed gently toward Shirburn Hill. I passed a couple of people out for a stroll. First one jogger, then another, passed me on the trail. Further down the path, the second man crossed paths with me, now heading in the opposite direction.

The path opened up, becoming a broad, grassy track bordered by trees on both sides with a dirt path running down the middle. I could hear the noisy M40 motorway up ahead, and before long, I passed underneath it, through a short tunnel.

The trail was easy going and mostly flat, and I continued at my brisk pace, passing a sign for the Aston Rowant Nature

Reserve on the right. The reserve is 392 acres in size (159 hectares), most of which is a biological Site of Special Scientific Interest, which denotes a protected natural area. Aston Rowant is a chalk grassland home to a variety of orchids, butterflies, and perhaps most importantly, the red kite, a bird that was formerly extinct in England before being reintroduced to this very nature reserve in 1989.

Shortly after, I saw a sign for a water tap within the reserve, just off the Ridgeway and visible from the trail. The tap was not mentioned in my guidebook, so it made for a pleasant surprise. But it was a chilly morning, and I had more than enough water, so I kept going without refilling my reserves. I seemed to be making good time, and I thought I might make the 11:30 train if I continued to hustle.

Today was the first day that I had started my walk focused on arriving at a destination rather than being fully present in the experience of the journey itself. The past couple of days, I had been tired toward the end of the walk, focused mostly on arriving. But for the primary part of the journey, I had been present in the moment. My mind was on one track today: get to Chinnor in time for the train.

I passed by quiet country lanes and other paths and continued straight on the Ridgeway. Sooner than I expected, I saw a village off in the distance that looked like it might be Chinnor. My guidebook had mentioned that a new housing development at the edge of the village that could be seen from the Ridgeway. I checked my watch. It couldn't be; I was too far ahead of schedule to be approaching Chinnor this early.

Before long, I began to catch glimpses of the old Chinnor chalk quarry down both sides of the Ridgeway. They were massive pits with very steep sides, with brilliant turquoise water glowing in the bottom of each of the pits. There were now fences along either side of the trail bearing NO TRES- PASSING signs and warning of the danger of falling into the deep pits, which looked impossible to climb out of. I couldn't imagine how a rescue mission would be handled. I passed a sign for a lost dog and hoped he hadn't fallen into one of the pits. If there were ever a place to keep your dog on a leash when walking, it was here.

I kept going until I reached a road, where I turned left for Chinnor, incredulous that I had arrived this early. I knew from my guidebook that the rail station was near the Ridgeway, well before the village itself. After just a few minutes, I saw a sign indicating that the rail station was off to the left, and I followed a quiet street where I saw a car park and then signs indicating where to buy tickets. An old train car was waiting at the station.

As I had discovered the evening before, the day's train was No. 1198, Linda the Lymington Flyer, one of only three complete units of its type left in the world. The unit was operated in push-pull mode with a Class 08 locomotive No. 08825, which will inevitably mean something to any train enthusiasts reading this book. Linda is an electric unit, but there is no third rail along this route to pick up electricity from, hence the need for the locomotive. Linda had been restored thanks to the efforts of the EMU Preservation Society, a registered charity dedicated to the preservation and restoration of third-rail electric multiple unit trains that once operated on the former Southern Region of British Rail. They have a team of volunteers who restore and operate the trains.

This registered charity is not alone in such an endeavor. The Chinnor & Princes Risborough Railway Association focuses on the restoration of this portion of the line, and they operate the railway on weekends throughout most of the year. They also hold special events such as cream teas on the trains, fish and chips quiz nights (yes, they serve food on the train), and the Ghoulish Scream & Steam for Halloween. They seem to be quite an active group, helping to educate people about the historic trains.

I quickly purchased a ticket and was informed that it was valid all day, meaning that I could ride back and forth as many times as I liked. The first departure, at 11:10, was a short 12-minute journey to Wainhill and back. I settled into a seat with my pack alongside me. There were a few other people in the carriage, but the train wasn't even half full. We rode down to Wainhill, stopping before heading back to the station. The train was slow going, and it was easy to enjoy the view of the Ridgeway from my window. A volunteer went through with a refreshment cart, and most of the other passengers took advantage of this opportunity to enjoy a cup of tea.

I stayed on for the next journey, which departed at 11:30 for Thame Junction, a 50-minute return trip. This was the departure that was initially scheduled for Princes Risborough, but that route had unfortunately been delayed to the 2:20 pm departure time. I was disappointed that I would miss the one to Princes Risborough that I had hustled all morning to arrive for, but I was excited to take a break from the trail to travel on an old train, whatever its destination. This was certainly not something I had expected when I first planned my historic Ridgeway walk: my focus had been on the much older historical sites I had left behind on the western section of the trail.

I noticed that as we passed a road junction, there was a young man alongside the tracks with red and green flags to signal to the train as to whether it was safe to cross the road or not. Manually operated gates separated the street from the tracks. It was all very quaint, and it was evident that real train enthusiasts ran the railway. Two of the young men who were checking tickets and counting passengers sat in the seats behind me on the return journey, excitedly talking about model trains.

After a very relaxing journey, we were once again back at Chinnor station, and I departed the train, opting not to stay on any longer. According to my calculations, I had just two more hours on the trail left that day, and I was in no rush at all to arrive. This approach to my journey was in stark contrast to my morning hustle to get to the train. By my estimation, I probably could have stayed for the 2:20 pm train to Princes Risborough and would still have made it to my B&B that afternoon by 6 pm. A third trip seemed excessive, though, so I quickly browsed through the gift shop, which was packed with train memorabilia and books, and then headed straight back to the Ridgeway.

It was about 12:30 by the time I reached the trail, and I soon saw a park off to the left, where I stopped to have my sandwich and air my feet, which were hot and tired. I was disappointed to see that I was starting to get blisters—probably due to my morning speed-walk. I was simultaneously pleased that I had made it until the sixth day without blisters and disappointed that I hadn't managed to walk the entire trail without getting one.

I dedicated a few minutes to my blister care. Then I changed my socks and headed back on the trail down a shady path lined with trees, which climbed gently upwards. I decided it was time to reconnect with Richard 2, and I pulled out my phone to begin recording. "Patience, patience, patience. Patience with yourself." These words were to become a mantra for me on my Ridgeway walk—the words of Richard 2 would return to my thoughts many times along the trail. "Know that as long as you are taking action based on the things that you know and feel are right for you, and the things that your intuition and your gut confirm are right for you, you are headed in the right direction. You are frustrated still that you have not been moving as fast as you would like, but you have been taking action; you have changed.

"Now I know that you want to show certain people in your life that you are a big name, that you are recognized, that you are known." Richard 2 was right, I am embarrassed to say.

There are certain people in my life that I still feel like I have to impress. "These are not the right motivations," Richard 2 reminded me, though I already knew this. "This is not the right motivation to be doing your work. You need to come from the heart, not from a place of proving yourself to someone. Come from the heart, take actions from the heart, and have patience with yourself, and you will be on your way. You are on your way. Trust the process.

"You have heard that before this week, and now today is the day of self-reliance. Know that you can take care of yourself no matter what, and everything you do now is part of the process of getting you to a point of self-sufficiency and, eventually, financial freedom. You will get the house that you want; you will get the lifestyle that you want. Patience, patience, patience. Patience with yourself. Patience, patience, patience. Patience with yourself.

"You keep this recording," said Richard 2. After writing down my sparse notes from the previous day, I decided that the most effective way to record their messages was on my phone. "You know it will be useful. You perhaps make a meditation with the teachings of Richard." I liked this idea; Cara Wilde, one of my most experienced channeling friends, has recorded meditations that she's channeled from one of her guides. I was excited at the thought of being able to do something similar with these new guides of mine.

I decided it was enough channeling for the day. Shortly after I put my phone away, I saw an unexpected sign for some barrows off to the right, which I decided to explore since they were supposedly just .4 mile (.64 km) off the trail. I walked steadily uphill, through what appeared to be another one of Grim's Ditches until I reached a point where the trail split into two. It had been about a half-mile, and there was no sign of barrows anywhere. I couldn't imagine where they might be.

I considered heading on but decided to conserve energy

and turn back, reminding myself of my blisters and the nonexistent stone circle on my first day near Avebury. According to my calculations, I had very little left on the trail that day, but I didn't want to waste too much time on a route that might end up being the completely wrong direction: one of the paths headed upward; the other wound downhill. It was impossible to know which way the barrows were located. I turned and went straight back to the Ridgeway, deciding that I had seen my share of tumuli on the western section of the trail, so I wasn't missing out on much.

Once back on the Ridgeway, the trail wound around a bit through the trees before heading straight. I was starting to get a little tired and pulled out my guidebook. There was a bench not far ahead, and I planned to rest there. Today was a short day of walking, but I was tired from the two previous days, which had been long ones. Plus, I had spent all morning hustling to get to Chinnor, and my feet weren't happy with the blisters.

The route crossed a quiet road, then continued before climbing steeply to the top of Lodge Hill. The path was now a pretty, grassy trail, with views all around. I stepped aside to let a jogger pass, and we greeted each other as he went by. He was wearing a number sign indicating that he was participating in some Ridgeway Challenge, which I later learned was a trail run of the entire Ridgeway over two days. That's right: the runners covered in two days what I was walking in eight. Their effort put my own into perspective.

I passed through a gate into the woods, and a few minutes later saw the bench to the left. I settled in, setting my pack alongside me and taking off my shoes and socks. A man walked by with a young girl and continued onward. As I rested, more people went past me, running along the trail behind my bench. Some were running, some walking, as they were coming up the other side of the hill. The Ridgeway Challengers were doing the route in the opposite direction, from east to west, and it looked like this was where I'd be crossing paths with the bulk of them.

When my feet were ready, I got back on the trail. I was tired, and my feet ached, and all I wanted at this point was to arrive at Princes Risborough. It was not yet 2 pm, and I was confused about how much time I had left on the trail that day: I had initially thought I'd arrive by 3 pm, but it now looked like it might be later.

I walked down the steep trail as it descended Lodge Hill, with runners passing me as they ascended the hill. They looked tired already, and they had a very long way to go before they reached Overton Hill. I had been walking the trail for six days now, and they were planning to run it in about 24 hours, nonstop. It was exhausting just to think about it.

From here, the Ridgeway ran directly through many cornfields before cutting through a golf course. Fortunately, this was another protected path bordered by trees, and I could see the fairways through gaps in the greenery. The trail came out across a level railway crossing and then headed uphill before crossing yet another rail line, over the tunnel's top. I knew I was close to Princes Risborough, yet it didn't feel close enough. I checked my guidebook and saw that I was finally on the last map of the day in my guide, which ended with the turnoff to the town.

The Ridgeway came straight down alongside a large house, then down a flat path and out onto the A4010 road, where I turned left. I was passing small groups of runners every few minutes. I continued down the narrow sidewalk toward town before turning right on Upper Icknield Way, where the Ridgeway continued past some homes, and then headed down a stony track that skirted the town. Would I ever make it to my accommodation?

I pulled out my guidebook to confirm I was in the right place and that I hadn't missed my turnoff for the town. It appeared that I was still on the right track. My feet were aching, and all I wanted was to find the George & Dragon on the High Street. I was so thankful I was walking at my own pace, and not running a race, like the people I had seen earlier. I passed a school, then continued until the Ridgeway came out on New Road, where I turned left to head into town. I was almost there.

I soon saw a bench off to the side of the road and was tempted to make one final stop before arriving. I was so tired that I couldn't imagine walking another fifteen minutes without a break. I pulled out my iPhone and checked the distance on Google Maps: it was just six minutes to my night's accommodation, so I continued straight there without stopping, anxious for a cup of tea and a shower. My usual Ridgeway routine.

I walked down the High Street and into the George & Dragon, informing the woman at the bar that I had a room booked for the night. It was quiet. There were a couple of people in the pub having an afternoon pint. I was shown to my room: out the pub's back door and into a separate building, up the stairs and down a long hallway.

"You're aware that there's a disco tonight, aren't you?" asked the woman who showed me to my room. I stared at her in silence for a moment. No one had mentioned a disco, but then I had booked my room online a couple of months prior without speaking to anyone.

She didn't think there would be much of a problem with noise, though my room did have a window that looked out onto the pub's garden area in the courtyard. I couldn't wander around and find a different place to stay, so I resigned myself to deal with the situation. There weren't many options in Princes Risborough for accommodation, and I didn't have the energy to start searching.

My room was spacious and comfortable, and I went straight to the shower before putting on the kettle to make a cup of tea to drink as I washed my clothes. Once everything was clean, I settled in for a rest. I went down for dinner as soon as they started serving meals and had the best minted peas I had ever had to accompany my fish and chips. I was the first person to dinner, and I sat alone in the dining area.

After dinner, I wandered down the High Street to buy some food. I needed to get a sandwich for lunch and some extra things for breakfast, as the pub only offered orange juice and tiny boxes of cereal in the room. I was a bit shocked to hear that they didn't provide a full cooked breakfast, as I had never come across such a situation at any of the pubs or B&Bs I had stayed at before. This lack of a cooked breakfast on the trail was entirely new for me. But at this point, there was nothing to do but to make my own.

The town was quiet, and my journey to and from M&S was uneventful. I bought a sandwich and tomatoes for lunch the following day and some yogurt and blueberries for breakfast. The disco didn't start until after I'd settled in my room for the night, returning from my food shopping. The music was loud, and it felt like I was in the middle of the party. It was an old building, and the windows were hardly soundproof. I braced myself for a rough night's sleep.

And a rough night it was, with the disco going on until midnight. I went to bed later than I usually did on my walks, just before eleven, and woke up intermittently until the music eventually went off. Unfortunately, no music meant that I could hear all the drunken conversations from below, and sleep came on and off until the pub finally closed for the night. I made a mental note to bring earplugs in the future.

DAY 7: PRINCES RISBOROUGH TO TRING
12.4 MILES (20 KM)

I woke up in the morning feeling more tired than usual and apprehensive about the day's walk. I did my morning meditation exercises and went down the hallway to fetch my breakfast and lunch. Many of the B&Bs I had stayed at had a mini fridge in the room for milk and snacks, but this place had what appeared to be a small camping refrigerator out in the hallway. It was not very practical and, as I soon discovered, not very effective.

My food was barely cooler than room temperature. I decided to have the yogurt with the muesli for breakfast, but I didn't trust the milk to use on my cereal and left it there. I wasn't sure why the pub's owners hadn't bothered to purchase a standard mini fridge for guests, especially since cereal was the only breakfast option they provided. The room was certainly large enough to accommodate a small refrigerator.

I put together a big bowl of muesli, plain yogurt, and blueberries, knowing that it wouldn't fuel me up as well as a cooked breakfast usually did. And yet, it was a welcome change from all the eggs, bacon, and sausage I had been eating throughout my journey. I had a ham sandwich and a packet of cherry tomatoes for lunch, and half a container of blueberries left over that could serve as a snack. The positive side of a cereal breakfast meant that it was fast and easy: I was out of my room by 8:35, heading up the High Street and then New Road toward the Ridgeway.

The trail passed some playing fields off to the left, then turned right into another field, where the path headed uphill. It began drizzling slightly, then stopped almost as soon as it had started. This pattern would continue throughout the day: very light rain lasting just a couple of minutes, with long stretches of ominous clouds and dry weather. The trail shortly entered a more wooded area, with several flights of steps climbing the hill. I passed a bench, where I felt tempted to stop—there were so few benches on the Ridgeway—but I had barely started walking that morning, and I was conscious that I had a long day of walking ahead of me.

I had meticulously counted the estimated walking times in my guidebook the night before. There were two options: walk to Wigginton, where I could call for a taxi to my hotel near Tring, or walk straight to the hotel itself. I planned to wait and see how I felt. The estimated walking time to Wigginton was a wide range: anywhere between five and a half hours and eight and a quarter, and from six and a quarter to nine and a quarter to Pendley Manor. I had decided to estimate my arrival for 5:30, which would allow me to be pleasantly surprised if I arrived earlier.

It was a Sunday morning, and there were plenty of dog walkers out. The Ridgeway continued into the Whiteleaf Nature Preserve, where the trail passed Whiteleaf Cross, a cross-shaped chalk hill carving, and a single tumulus. The cross's date and origin are unknown, though there is mention of it as early as 1742. I was now clearly in the Chilterns, an affectionate term for the Chiltern Hills, which form a chalk escarpment. A large portion of the Chilterns was designated as an Area of Outstanding Natural Beauty in 1965.

The trail became a steep path heading downhill, which felt disappointing after putting in so much effort to climb the hill. It then led out into Cadsden, a tiny village that was home to The Plough pub, which of course, was closed on a Sunday morning. After a short walk down a quiet road and past The Plough, the Ridgeway headed back into nature, crossing a field before climbing yet another hill.

Once the path leveled out, it followed alongside a very sturdy metal fence that bore some very serious NO TRES-PASSING signs every few meters. The fence was unlike any I had ever seen before, and it took me some time before I realized I was walking along the edge of the Chequers property: the country house of the UK Prime Minister. That explained the heavy security.

The Ridgeway turned left off the main trail to cross through the Chequers property, passing through dried-up fields of some kind of bean crop before crossing the entrance driveway. I walked swiftly past security cameras, pointing in both directions. After the quiet remoteness of previous days on the Ridgeway, it was strange to be walking down a trail with such high levels of security, and I wondered why the National Trail hadn't been re-routed to go around the property, rather than straight through it.

As I exited Chequers through a gate, a couple passed me, asking if the path we were on was a circular trail. I told them I was on the Ridgeway, but I had seen signs for a circular walk on the signposts. They were concerned about heading off into nowhere and getting lost (they weren't dressed for an outdoor adventure), and it was still drizzling on and off. I had no idea just how long the circular trail was, so I left them to continue on their path. Later research showed that the Coombe Hill and Chequers trail is 5-7 miles long. It's more of a figure-eight shape than a circle, meaning that the route can be cut short at 5 miles or extended to the full 7 miles.

I knew from my guidebook that there was a bench up ahead on the trail, and I forged on, wanting to reach that milestone before taking a rest. I turned out onto a quiet lane and passed the Buckmoorend Farm Shop, an unexpected attraction. There were signs announcing tea and cake, and I felt a bit hungry, but I decided to hold out for the benches further on. I had my lunch with me and did not need to add to it.

It was here that I got lost. There was a branching of trails, and I took the wrong one. Fortunately, I didn't get far before realizing I probably wasn't heading the right way and turned around. I asked two women on horses if they knew which of the trails was the Ridgeway, and, surprisingly, they didn't. One of their horses sounded distressed, snorting and fussing so loudly that I had first heard him when I was on the other trail, and they excused themselves and backtracked down to the road toward the farm.

Seconds after, I saw a sign that seemed to indicate where the trail led, and at the same time, I saw a couple of dog walkers heading down the path toward me. I asked them if we were on the Ridgeway, and they confirmed that we were. I then headed confidently uphill into woodland. Because I had my mind on the benches ahead, the shady woodland trail seemed to go on forever. But it shortly came out onto a road, where I turned right and then soon turned again off the road before coming out into an open area. The right-hand side of the trail remained wooded. Off to the left, there was a wide-open view of the countryside below.

Most importantly, there was a bench. It had started to drizzle again, and the trees didn't protect the it. I sat down on the wet wood anyway, pulling out the leftover blueberries and eating them all. I followed by eating half of my sandwich and then a handful of cherry tomatoes. Some day walkers went by, bundled up in their waterproof jackets as I sat there in my thin t-shirt, not bothered by the rainfall. It was far too hot to put waterproofs on, and it was barely raining at all.

After several minutes, the precipitation slowed to a light mist, and I decided it was in my best interest to air out my feet and eventually change my socks. I relaxed on the bench as my feet cooled in the air. When I felt that they were ready to head back on the trail, I put on a new pair of socks, placed the old pair in the mesh pocket of my backpack for them to dry out, and headed off on the Ridgeway.

It was rough going for the first few minutes after the break. My muscles had cooled down, and I hobbled along stiffly and awkwardly before finally warming up again. I passed several more benches on my right as I approached a large monument on Coombe Hill's corner. It was a popular spot to enjoy the view, and I could see a small group of people were at the memorial, gazing off at distant sights through binoculars.

The Coombe Hill Monument, a Grade II Listed monument, was erected in 1904 in memory of the 148 men from Buckinghamshire who died during the Second Boer War. The monument is significant not because it was constructed to commemorate a great victory but rather to remember those killed in the war. In front of the monument is another trig point topped with a plaque pointing to several distant features in the landscape, including Ivinghoe Beacon, the endpoint on the Ridgeway. I traced my fingers along the line and stared out in the distance toward the point I would reach the following day.

I turned right, following the Ridgeway along a footpath, which eventually led down the side of Bacombe Hill. There was a chalky ditch to the left, and the trail transformed into a slippery slide down a white, chalky path as it approached a gate leading out onto a road. Because it had been raining throughout the day, and the chalk was smooth, I slipped twice as I went down the trail, letting out a yelp the second time. It was thanks to my Pacerpoles that I was able to stay on my feet and not fall. I turned around to see another walker not far behind me, and we discussed how slippery the trail had become due to the chalk surface. As we approached the gate, there were bits of grass alongside the path that we could gingerly walk along to gain some traction. I had grown so used to the Ridgeway's easy terrain that this little hill of chalk was a surprise.

After that, the Ridgeway headed down a road past Wendover station and then continued straight through the village. I stopped to sit on a wet bench on the High Street to check my map, and a man walked past, pausing to ask if I was doing the whole Ridgeway. I said that I was, and he seemed impressed. He indicated where to follow the trail out of the village, and I headed in that direction, eventually seeing the Ridgeway sign alongside the road.

My next landmark for a rest stop was a church: St. Mary the Virgin, in Wendover. I was a bit apprehensive about stopping at a church since it was a Sunday, and there would undoubtedly be people everywhere, but I had grown accustomed to my tradition of resting in churchyards. They were quiet and peaceful (except on Sundays), and they always had benches. I passed down a narrow alleyway and then through a park, which was full of places to sit. I considered stopping to rest here, and not at the church. I decided to continue, walking past all the benches before I eventually came out in front of the church.

It was just past noon, and I could see from the sign that the last service had begun at 10:30. Some people were still leaving the church, and I walked up its main pathway and sat on a bench near the entrance. I pulled off my pack and took out the second half of my sandwich to eat, following it with a handful of cherry tomatoes.

Everyone greeted me as they departed, and one woman

suggested I rest inside where it was warmer, but I was too wet and muddy, and I didn't want to enter the church in that condition. I was also concerned about taking off my shoes to air out my feet. I had no qualms about doing that if I were all alone in an empty churchyard, but it didn't seem right with people still departing after the morning service. I was starting to think I would have been better off resting in the park.

Before long, I got up, pulled my pack back on, and headed off down the Ridgeway, which ran alongside the churchyard before gently climbing another hill. After I reached the top, a small group of cyclists whizzed by me, racing down the hill. They were the last people I saw until almost an hour later.

From here, the Ridgeway wound through woods along a soft, easy trail through Barn Wood and later Hale Wood, eventually coming out onto a road alongside a farm before once more heading back into the forest. Here, the footpath followed the bottom of a ditch. A couple of cyclists awkwardly crossed the ditch ahead of me, climbing down one side with their cycles and then back up the other side.

Eventually, the trail came out of the woods onto a road, which I crossed before heading into an open field. It had been about an hour since my last break at the church. There was no sign of a bench—not in my guidebook or on the actual trail—so I sat down in the grass next to a hedgerow and took off my pack. I ate a handful of cherry tomatoes and drank some water.

Here, I was free to give my feet the rest they were asking for, and I rested there. I changed socks and evaluated how much farther I had to go. It appeared that I was making excellent time on the trail that day, which was a pleasant surprise. I was still debating on how to get to my hotel. I remained resolved to decide upon arriving in Wigginton, the nearest village where I could call for a taxi.

I got up, pulled my pack on, and crossed an open field, heading in the general direction of a communications tower off in the distance. There was a signpost halfway down the field marked with the National Trail acorn, and I walked toward it and then past it toward the tower. After crossing yet another quiet country road, the Ridgeway entered Pavis Wood.

My were thankful for the break, but they were still aching, and I wanted to try to walk to the hotel if I could. I stopped alongside the trail and took two ibuprofens, unsure if they would help the foot ache but thinking it was worth a try. It didn't quite make sense, but somehow it worked. My feet still hurt a little, but my muscles felt better, and walking became more comfortable.

I decided it was time to reconnect with Richard 3, and I pulled out my phone to record. His message began: "You have seen what can happen when you ask people for help. They are happy to help you. This is easy to do. This is time to create something and ask for help from people to promote it. It could be your online course; it could be upgrading your online course. Something like this challenge that you've done with Lisa [I had recently run a month-long program with my coach Lisa], learn how to perhaps team up with other people in the future."

He mentioned the names of two of my business friends. "Think of these people that you would like to team up with and do something with them. This gives you each exposure to the other person's audience. You've known this. This is a joint venture. It's time for you to do more of these. More of these. This will help you create financial stability. You've also thought today of creating a paperback with the content of your existing four business books; this is a good idea. Creating these things— these products—will help create financial stability.

"You're putting yourself out there in a much bigger way. You finally understand this. This is good. And the more you do this, the bigger you get, the more visible you get, the more financial stability you will have. You are reminded of Sanaya Roman's guided meditation with Orin; this is appropriate. You can listen to them every night if you so choose. They are good for you. Good for you to attract people, to magnetize yourself so that people come to you. You know also that it is time for you to create a new opt-in gift because, as you have learned, they expire. Some people can get by with having one for so long," said Richard 3, mentioning a business friend of mine. He continued: "but she has also gotten by with a very old website that does not represent her, so you cannot compare yourself to other people. You see that your opt-in does not work, you give it away for free, and you create another one."

This advice ended up being excellent. Not long after returning from my Ridgeway walk, I went through all the opt-in gifts I had on my website, weeding out the ones that had not been very popular. I made them available for free: I put old guided meditations up on my YouTube channel, and I cleaned up my free Resources page on my website. It felt good to declutter the things that weren't working for me.

Richard 3 continued: "You see how you can incorporate contents from that giveaway into a book that perhaps you can sell. This is the way. Because for you, financial stability equals visibility. Visibility equals financial stability. You know this is an issue for you because you have written a book on it [my Business Visibility book]. You know this is an issue for you because your clients come to you with this issue. This is your big thing. So many people talk about visibility, but how visible are they really?"

He referenced two of my business friends who specialized in business visibility: "Your friend Jessica [name changed], how visible is she? Your friend Olivia [name also changed], how visible is she? They are not visible: big, big, big time visible. This is what you want, and this is what you can achieve, and this is important because you can help others overcome their issues around visibility. You are good at this; you are known for this; this is important. Visibility equals stability; stability equals visibility. You know this. You must focus on this. Yes, yes, make a sign. Make a sign. Shine. Make a shine, make a sign." Sometimes it felt like the Richards enjoyed playing with words. "Visibility equals stability, stability equals visibility, and you know when you speak of stability, you speak of financial stability. This is how it is. You know this. You know this. All these things that we tell you are things that you already know. We just do the service of pointing them out to you. We point them out. We point them out."

Richard 3 was right: everything that they had said thus far made absolute sense, and they weren't telling me anything that I didn't already know. They were just pointing out things that I wasn't paying attention to—and then repeating them over and over, like a mantra, so that I wouldn't forget them. "Visibility equals stability; stability equals visibility" were words that would also repeat in my mind throughout my Ridgeway walk.

And they were right about the visibility thing. That was my biggest challenge when building my business: getting over my fear of being visible when marketing my business online. It was also the biggest challenge that my clients came to me with, and it was no surprise that it was the topic of my third business book, Business Visibility.

I finished channeling as I came out onto a quiet lane, totally unsure which way to go. It wasn't entirely clear from my guidebook, and the fingerpost sign wasn't pointing in either direction but kind of in the middle. I turned right and realized it would probably be best to check and see if I had a signal on my phone before going too far. I did, and I confirmed via Google Maps that I was going in the wrong direction, as I had suspected.

I backtracked to the Ridgeway and continued down the lane in the other direction, toward Hastoe. I passed two cyclists who were also lost. They were cycling the Ridgeway from east to west and hadn't brought a map. They had forgotten it at home!

I pulled out my guidebook and explained where to find the turnoff to head into the woods. It wasn't until later that I realized that they probably wouldn't be able to cycle through most of the trail I had passed that day as much of it was footpaths, not bridleways. Unlike the South Downs Way, which can be traversed by walkers, cyclists, and riders for its full length of 100 miles, the Ridgeway had sections, particularly in the eastern half, which were only suitable for walkers. I wondered how much research they had done in planning their trip. Not much, from the looks of it.

The trail continued down Hastoe's Church Lane for a few minutes. I was hungry again and pulled my last apple out of my bag and ate it as I walked. The importance of having a cooked breakfast before starting on the trail each morning was apparent: this was the only morning that I hadn't had one, and I was hungrier than usual. The trail turned left down Marlin Hill, then right into Tring Park, a clear sign that I was getting very close to my final destination for the day.

The trail through Tring Park was a mile long, down a wide, flat path lined with shady trees. Many other people were out for an afternoon walk through the park: couples and families, with and without dogs. After so many days on the Ridgeway, this portion of the trail had a decidedly urban feel. The mile was over soon enough, and the trail exited the park and crossed a road to enter Wigginton. There were just about 45 minutes left on the trail, and without giving it much thought, I forged on toward my hotel.

There was a short path between fields before the Ridgeway crossed a long bridge over the busy A41. This road was the biggest I had seen all week, and it was a bit shocking after the peaceful, remote feeling of the rest of the Ridgeway. The trail crossed another road before continuing straight on down a path with fences on either side. Trees lined the route on the left; fields lay beyond the fence on the right.

My feet were hurting again. There was a very tender area on the sole of my right foot, right in between my big toe and the one next to it. It couldn't be a blister, not in that area, but it certainly hurt. I started walking unevenly, hobbling along as the pain worsened.

The trail came out onto a road, where I turned left before reaching another one. It was here that the Ridgeway continued right, past Tring Station. But that would have to wait for tomorrow. I turned left to head toward Pendley Manor, where I was staying the night. As I slowly and awkwardly approached the turnoff to the hotel, I felt a sharp pain in my right foot, which then subsided a bit. I was grateful for this, but I couldn't imagine what had happened. It almost felt like a blister had burst, and the pain and pressure had been released. I was very close to arriving at that night's accommodation, and I focused on reaching it soon.

I was concerned about booking a stay at Pendley Manor, as it didn't seem very walker friendly. I had initially booked at The Greyhound in Wigginton, but due a glitch in their reservations system, they had canceled mine. I had scrambled to find an alternative. The upside was that Pendley Manor was located very close to the Ridgeway, even closer than I had realized when I booked, but the downside was that it was a large hotel, spa, and event center that specialized in weddings.

This last detail became even more apparent as soon as I walked in the door. The hotel was busy, and wedding guests were everywhere, all dressed up for the event. There were not one but two parties at the hotel that afternoon. This was not the type of place I usually stayed at on my walks, and it was certainly not the kind of hotel I was comfortable walking into while looking like a sweaty mess.

I checked in at the front desk, where the receptionist suggested I use the porter to carry my bag up to the room. I turned around and looked at him, all decked out in his uniform. This level of formality was most decidedly not part of my usual accommodation on a walking holiday. After carrying my bag over 80 miles down the Ridgeway, it would be ridiculous to get help with my pack up the stairs to my room. I made a joke to that effect, thanked them both, and wandered down the hallway to find the stairs up to my room.

Like many hotels that have been established in old manor houses, the place was a labyrinth. Eventually, I found my room and settled in. It was large, with a huge bathroom, and was comfortable enough, though everything looked old and tired—like it hadn't been renovated since the 1950s. The hotel seemed to mirror how I felt.

After I showered and changed, I inspected my feet. There was nothing new to see, and there was certainly no hint of what had happened on my right foot: there was no apparent blister and no other type of injury. It all looked very much as it had in the morning when I had set off.

Once that was sorted, I began to worry about dinner. My guidebook indicated that "smart casual" was appreciated in the dining room. My evening clothes were nothing of the sort, and I knew I looked more like "outdoors casual," which I didn't think would be appreciated. I considered getting room service, but after reading through the hotel information booklet, I found a more relaxed venue for meals and snacks in the hotel's Shakespeare Bar. After fully resting, I grabbed my iPad and room card and headed down for an early dinner.

The bar was full of people, but it had a much more relaxed feel to it than the rest of the hotel, and most of the people there were reasonably quiet. Small round tables were dotted throughout the room, surrounded by comfortable looking chairs. I settled into a table in the far corner, next to the bar, away from the others.

I was starving, and I decided on the chicken breast with creamed Cashel Blue sauce and a glass of wine. It was my last dinner on the trail, and I had that nostalgic feeling that I had experienced on the South Downs Way: my journey was coming to an end, and I was sad to be returning to the real world. It was always difficult to leave the magic of the trail and return to everyday life, especially on the longer routes.

After I had eaten, I relaxed at my table with my wine and continued to type up the day's events on my iPad. When the waiter came around and asked if I wanted any dessert, I surprised myself by ordering some. I rarely indulged. I was still hungry, and I didn't want my last dinner to end because once it did, it meant that I was that much closer to wrapping up my time on the Ridgeway.

I finished typing up this day's chapter and got up from my table to return to my room, where I rested a bit before finally going to bed. I had a very short day ahead of me, which meant that I did not need to rush to get ready in the morning. I could sleep in and have a leisurely breakfast.

DAY 8: TRING TO IVINGHOE BEACON
5.1 MILES (8 KM)

Because this was such a short day on the trail, I set my alarm for a full hour later than usual, at 8:00. I got up, did my morning meditation exercises, then headed downstairs for a leisurely meal. Unfortunately, I could linger only so long, and the breakfast room was full of people, which still felt uncomfortable after so many quiet days on the Ridgeway. It rained a bit as I ate, which surprised me, as rain hadn't been in the forecast for the day. It was a reminder that you can never really trust the British weather forecast—even in the summer.

After I finished my breakfast, I went back upstairs and immediately checked the weather report: cloudy for the first few hours, then sunny the rest of the afternoon. It had stopped raining, and fortunately, it didn't start back up again during my short walk that day. I put everything together, arranging my things in my pack for the last time that week. I filled my one-liter bottle with water for my head in case I needed cooling off, and I checked my pouch: just about a liter and a half of water, more than enough for the day ahead.

I checked out of Pendley Manor and walked down the long

drive back to the road. As I approached the Ridgeway, I saw that I was about to cross the Grand Union Canal, and I took a quick detour down some steps to see the narrow boats along the canal. The Grand Union Canal runs for 137 miles from London to Birmingham, and with all of its branches, it is by far the longest canal in the UK, at 286.3 miles total. It was cool and shady by the water, but there was no point in lingering here. I took some photos and headed back up toward the Ridgeway. I had about three miles (just under 5 km.) to walk to the end of the trail.

I passed Tring rail station, then its car park, and continued down the road, crossing it to turn up a concrete track. The Ridgeway then departed the trail as it turned left. Thankfully my guidebook had clear directions, as there was no sign to indicate that the Ridgeway departed from the visible track. The trail retreated into nature down a tree-lined footpath that rose steadily toward Ivinghoe Beacon.

A dog galloped up alongside me from behind, and I greeted him before looking back to see his owner jogging along the path. Further on, I passed a woman walking in the opposite direction to me. It was a relatively quiet morning on the trail, despite it being a bank holiday Monday. I decided it was time to reconnect with Richard 4.

"Patience, patience, patience. Patience with the process. Return to your habit, your practice of identifying the three most important tasks every day. At least one of these tasks should be something to make you more visible and to get you more visible and to get you out there more. This is very important. Return to that process as part of your new morning ritual, which you have discussed with the other Richards. Patience with the process. Take steps to put yourself out there and make yourself more visible. Enjoy the process. Look at it as a game. Like the games you are playing for memory." I had recently started using Brainwell, a brain-training app, in the hopes of improving my memory.

"See if you can set yourself little goals for visibility and achieve them. Ask Kerri how soon is too soon to pitch to the podcasts again and consider doing that in some time. This is an important part of the process." I had worked with a PR expert earlier in the month to pitch myself to be a guest on other business podcasts and was curious how long I had to wait before contacting the ones who hadn't responded. The Richards were giving practical advice, which I appreciated.

I finished my channeling as I passed a sign for the Aldbury Nowers Nature Reserve, the first of many I would pass that morning. The reserve is a 19.7-hectare biological Site of Special Scientific Interest, and its chalk grassland is home to several different butterfly species. There was a bench to the right of the path, just before some woodland stairs, which I ignored. The trail continued through the trees, rising steadily.

The Ridgeway soon leveled out at the top of Pitstone Hill and became a wide, grassy path with sweeping views. I could see the dark turquoise water of the old chalk pit down to the left, with Ivinghoe Beacon off in the far distance ahead and hills to all sides. It was strange to finally have the end of the Ridgeway in sight, and I felt that familiar twinge of sadness that my journey was about to come to a close.

A pickup truck came up the hill in front of me, passing me by as I stepped to the side. It was an unexpected sighting on the trail. I couldn't figure out what it was doing up there, randomly driving around. There didn't seem to be any fields or farm animals to check on.

The Ridgeway continued down the other side of the hill, then through a car park, and crossed a road before continuing in the same direction. There were more people on the trail now, walking in both directions. The sun was out, and families were taking advantage of the holiday. It reminded me of my final day on the South Downs Way, particularly that last busy stretch along the Seven Sisters, where the increase in foot traffic along the Way helped ease me back into the reality of life off the trail. Nonetheless, I couldn't help but wish it weren't a bank holiday so that I could have a quieter end to my adventure. I made a mental note to plan things better in the future.

The Ridgeway continued ahead as a broad, grassy track with fields to the right side. It headed steadily up Steps Hill (which, interestingly, lacked in steps). There were more and more day walkers out now, mostly couples and families. The trail wound around and down to a road, which it crossed before approaching Beacon Hill. I walked slowly, not wanting to rush my arrival.

The path then headed steeply up the hill. Families were everywhere, walking both uphill and downhill. Many of them were carrying kites and model planes. There was a steep shortcut to the top of the hill, which I ignored in favor of continuing up the official Ridgeway trail. I wanted no shortcuts on this end to my journey. Eventually, I came out on top of the hill and approached the information board, which had a full map of the Ridgeway trail. That was all there was indicating the end of the journey; there was no "87 miles to Overton Hill" sign pointing the opposite direction.

It was all a bit overwhelming, even though all the foot traffic on the trail should have prepared me for a crowd at the top of Ivinghoe Beacon. I sat down on the edge of the hill, looking off into the distance at the views around me and resting my feet. I turned off airplane mode on my phone, which I had turned on to conserve battery, and posted some Instagram photos that I had taken along my walk that day.

It was a bit of an anticlimactic end to a long walk, but I had anticipated that after my South Downs Way experience the previous year. Still, I felt the need to tell people around me—or at the very least, one person—that I had just completed an 87-

mile walk. It was like I wanted some form of recognition for my accomplishment. That would have been awkward, though, so I kept it to myself.

I got up, approached the information board once again, and asked a man with two little girls to take a photograph of me next to the Ridgeway map. That satisfied my need for completion. Then I was off, backtracking one mile on the trail to a point where I had seen a sign indicating another path toward the village of Ivinghoe. According to my guidebook, there was a "very steep faint path" down the side of Beacon Hill that would save me a mile on the walk to Ivinghoe, but I couldn't find it. Perhaps it was the shortcut I had seen earlier. I resolved to continue down the main trail, as I felt like I had enough energy in me to walk two miles rather than one to the Rose & Crown pub in Ivinghoe, where I would wait to be picked up by my husband.

My foot was still hurting, so I walked as quickly as I could back to the fingerpost sign indicating the trail to Ivinghoe, then continued swiftly down the flat, grassy path toward the village. It was a much quieter trail, and I passed only a couple of people along the way. I soon reached the village of Ivinghoe, walking down a busy road until I saw the turnoff toward my destination.

Once I arrived in Ivinghoe, it was easy to find the Rose & Crown, which thankfully was quiet inside. Most people seemed to be enjoying their meals in the garden. But after so many days out in the open sun, I felt the need to relax in the shade. Once again, I was ready for some time indoors. I settled in to write this last chapter of my walk on my iPad.

I now had another National Trail under my belt, and I had learned a great deal about myself and my walking preferences along the way. My 87-mile Ridgeway walk had been much, much easier than my South Downs Way experience. There were ups and downs, but the difficult parts were nothing compared to what I had experienced on the South Downs. My past experience on the South Downs Way and my two Downs Link walks had made the Ridgeway a much easier experience. So much so that I was already looking forward to my next long walk, which I had decided would be the Dales Way. I had barely completed my Ridgeway journey, and I was already eager for more.

EPILOGUE

When reviewing all the chapters that I had written each evening while walking the Ridgeway, I was struck by the massive difference in tone from my first long-distance walking experience, the South Downs Way. My Ridgeway experience was so much easier than my South Downs walk, and it was easy to see why.

For one, I walked the 87-mile trail in eight days, the same amount of time I took to walk the 100 miles of the South Downs. That made for shorter days: fewer hours of walking each day, more time to enjoy the sites, and making as many rest stops as I liked. The weather was just as hot and sunny on the Ridgeway as it had been on the South Downs, but I learned the secret to staying cool: drenching my head with water.

Much like my South Downs experience, I relished the feeling that my time on the trail was like being in another world, or another dimension, separate somehow from ordinary reality, even though I ended up in a village or small town every night to sleep. Part of this magic, I believe, comes from walking the trail alone and allowing myself to enter that deep state of mobile meditation as I walked each day. I'm sure that channeling the Richards also helped.

If you've read my book *Alone on the South Downs Way*, you may remember that I pulled an oracle card for each day of my journey. Interestingly, though not surprisingly, each day's general theme corresponded to each day's oracle card. You may be wondering whether it was the same for the Ridgeway: I did, though each day's theme seemed to be much less important and play a much smaller role on each day of my journey. That's why I'm including this in the Epilogue—not throughout the book, as I did in my South Downs Way book.

Day 0: Miracle Healing

This day was my walk around Avebury and my discovery of West Kennet long barrow. I still feel the deep connection with that site that I had on my first visit. While I'm not sure whether I experienced miracle healing on Day 0 of my Ridgeway journey, I know that West Kennet was where I began to receive the first downloads of information about the new energy transformation process that I now use to work with clients. In meditation at West Kennet on a visit in late 2016, I received the symbol for my new healing method, as well as the first details of how it worked.

It's truly a life-changing process for me, having channeled and developed it, so perhaps Day 0 indeed was a day of miracle healing, even if I didn't see it at the time. It certainly sparked a connection with a particular location, which has become a special place for me, one I return to every other month. And the message I received this day from Richard 1—peace and space—coincides with the perfect ingredients for miracle healing.

Day 1: Inner Power

The message from Richard 2 was very much aligned with inner power. He said, "Patience, patience, patience. Patience with yourself." When I allow myself to be patient with myself and with my journey, it gives me an inner power that I miss when I'm rushing around and pressuring myself.

Richard 2 urged me to take risks because of the powerful growth that can result. And I think there's a lot of strength—inner power—that can come from risk-taking. It can teach us the power of stepping outside our comfort zone and trying new things. So, while I may not have experienced inner power on Day 1 of my journey, the messages were there.

Day 2: Trust Your Intuition

Intuition has been a theme for me in recent years, as I worked to reconnect with myself and learn to tap into the wisdom of my intuition. It's become so important to me that I wrote a book on it, Business Intuition. And perhaps trusting my intuition was more of a theme for the entire walk, rather than for this day precisely. However, I trusted my intuition when I made individual decisions on the trail, such as avoiding specific detours or making a stop at the Burj for cold water.

Richard 3's advice about financial stability was mostly practical action steps, rather than a nudge to trust my intuition.

Day 3: Vacation

"Patience, patience, patience. Patience with the process" was the theme of Richard 4's message for me on this day. If I look at my long-distance walking adventures as a vacation, then this makes sense. Patience with the process: enjoy the journey; don't focus on the destination. And perhaps it was on Day 3 that I truly sank into the depth of the solitary experience that is a solo long-distance walk.

Day 4: Romantic Partner

I have no clue what this message means. Day 4 was the day without Richards, and it was the long, solitary, uneventful portion of the Ridgeway. Nothing eventful happened when I spoke with Agustín in the evening, and this message still makes no sense to me. No changes on the horizon with our relationship? More of the same? I don't know.

Day 5: Honoring Your True Feelings

This day was a lovely one on the trail, with the morning featuring the cool Thames to my left and in the afternoon, a walk alongside Grim's Ditch, with two beautiful churches as a highlight. Day 5 was when Richard 1 urged me to create a personalized morning ritual that would give me peace of mind. Perhaps that would give me the space to tap into my true feelings so that I could honor them?

Day 6: Self Reliance

"Come from the heart, take actions from the heart, and have patience with yourself, and you will be on your way. You are on your way. Trust the process. You have heard that before this week, and now today is the day of self-reliance," said Richard 2. He specifically referenced the theme of the day in his message, so I suppose this is clear enough. "Know that you can take care of yourself no matter what, and everything you do now is part of the process of getting you to a point of self-sufficiency and, eventually, financial freedom. You will get the house that you want; you will get the lifestyle that you want. Patience, patience, patience. Patience with yourself."

Day 7: New Opportunity

This day was when Richard 3 gave me specific tips on how to create new opportunities: joint ventures in my business, a new book idea, new opt-in gifts. So while I didn't exactly experience a new opportunity while on the trail, I was given clear information on creating a new opportunity for myself.

Day 8: Awakening Your True Self

"Patience, patience, patience. Patience with the process," said Richard 4, which ties in so well with the day's theme. Solo long-distance walking is very much about awakening and connecting with my true self, and Richard's reminder to have patience with the process was perfect timing. I often get frustrated with myself: I see how far I have come in terms of personal development, yet I focus on how far I have yet to go. Richard's message was a good reminder that awakening one's true self is a journey, just like my Ridgeway walk.

IT'S NOW BEEN ALMOST a year since I walked the Ridgeway, and I so enjoyed reliving my experience as I worked on this book, with all the numerous rounds of writing and editing. I loved the Ridgeway, and it's a trail that I can imagine doing again. With the notable exception of Day 4, there are many fascinating historical and cultural features that make this route truly special.

My return from the Ridgeway was awkward, but that wasn't a surprise after my previous long-distance trails. It's always

strange to come home to everyday life after a few days in solitude out on a trail. But I think that the more I do it, the easier
the transition becomes. Before long, the soreness disappeared,
and the blisters peeled off my feet. I eventually discovered that
the pain in my left foot was indeed some strange blister that
was so deep that it appeared invisible to the naked eye, yet it
split and healed several days after I completed my journey.

The Ridgeway was every bit as magical as my South Downs
adventure, yet it was different in so many ways. I now understand more about what these experiences mean to me: it's the
challenge, the adventure, and the solitude that help me deepen
my connection with myself. It makes it easier to stick to my true
north so I can stay on track. It helps me strengthen my relationship with my intuition and make decisions more quickly and
easily. It gives me confidence. In short, a solitary long-distance
walk allows me become more me.

I hope you've enjoyed this journey, and I hope that this
book has encouraged you to try long-distance walking for yourself, whether it's on the Ridgeway, the South Downs Way, or
somewhere else. If you're new to long-distance trails, I highly
recommend a shorter route such as the Downs Link or the
Wey-South Path, both of which can be completed in two to
three days.—or in one day, if you're really ambitious! Solitary
walking in nature is truly life-changing, and it's an experience
that I invite you to try.

Happy walking!

PART II

EAST TO WEST

INTRODUCTION

In 2019, I walked the South Downs Way for the second time. It had been four years since the first time I had done the trail, and it was a completely different experience. It was wonderful, and I was so happy that I had revisited the route. It gave me a chance to update my book, Alone on the South Downs Way, and in 2020 I published the second edition of that book. I included the two routes, and compared and contrasted my two experiences, which were like night and day.

As soon as I finished my second South Downs journey, I knew I had to do the same with the Ridgeway. And so I planned to walk the trail, this time in the opposite direction (from east to west) in spring of 2021. My walking calendar was filled for 2020: I planned the Camino Portugués in March and the Camino Inglés in September or October.

And then COVID-19 happened. It felt so sudden, but in reality I should have seen it coming. I had been keeping an eye on updates on the Camino, and people were slowly leaving the trail to return home. But I was optimistic, and I thought it would all be over soon, and I would soon set foot on my first Camino adventure.

How wrong I was! I cancelled my Camino Portugués and I never even planned my Camino Inglés. The following year, 2021, would be a holy year in Santiago, and all the Caminos would be overcrowded. I decided to postpone any Caminos until 2022.

And so that left 2020. What to do? I was able to get away on a last-minute camping and walking trip throughout Wiltshire and West Sussex when I would have been on the Camino Portugués. Then lockdown hit, and that was the end of adventures away from home.

As the year progressed, the UK was in and out of lockdowns, and I didn't think I would be able to get in a single long-distance trail. But toward the end of the summer, restrictions were lifting, and I went on Booking.com to look at availability on the Ridgeway in September. I had grown used to booking my walking holidays at least three months in advance, but it looked like this year I might be able to get away with a last-minute reservation.

And so, I did. I resolved to walk the Ridgeway in the opposite direction, from Ivinghoe Beacon to my beloved Avebury, making for a more exciting end to my journey. Not only that, I would do it in one less day than I had in 2016. My fingers clicking rapidly on my laptop, I hurriedly reserved every single night on my seven-night journey.

And then I was done. It was set. It was confirmed. I was walking the Ridgeway again! I couldn't wait to get started.

My second Ridgeway adventure was even more magical than the first. I loved approaching the different sites from the opposite direction, and I relished the ease that came from being a more experienced long-distance walker. I'm so excited to share with you my new journey on the Ridgeway.

DAY 1

11.3 MILES (18.1 KM)

Whenever I walk a long-distance trail, it always feels abstract until the moment I'm actually on the route. Not so this time. I was so excited to get going on my second Ridgeway adventure that I was raring to go from Monday morning. Unfortunately, I had to wait until Wednesday to get started on my walk, as I had booked everything to start mid-week.

Because the northeastern terminus of the Ridgeway is in the middle of nowhere, my husband drove me there. We parked in the National Trust car park, and he walked up with me to my starting point at the top of Ivinghoe Beacon. It was exciting for me to return with him to this point because I had put together a route in this area for him to run and for me to walk a couple of months prior. We had, quite by chance, crossed paths right at Ivinghoe Beacon.

I hadn't realized on my first Ridgeway journey that Ivinghoe Beacon was a hill fort. It is a late Bronze Age to early Iron Age hill fort that was settled from the 7th-8th centuries BC. There's not much left of the ramparts, which probably explains why I hadn't noticed it. It's also roughly triangular, rather than rounded, as are many of the others.

Ivinghoe Beacon was initially thought to date back to the Iron Age, but further excavations, including pottery and artifact dating, later showed that it was occupied from the Late Bronze Age, with the earthwork ramparts dating to the Iron Age. There are numerous barrows around the site, which show just how much of a settlement was located here.

Agustín took some photos of me at the sign that marks the end (or the start, for me) of the trail; then we walked down Beacon Hill together to the point where I would continue along the Ridgeway, and he would head back to the car park, and then to London for a meeting. I stopped to pull off my fleece, as it was already too warm for it. I pulled my backpack on and continued on my journey. I was thrilled to be walking the trail again, but this time in the opposite direction: toward Avebury, a place that had become so special to me. It felt much more significant for me to walk toward Avebury rather than toward a random hill fort.

Even though it was a Wednesday morning, there were many walkers out as I worked my way down Steps Hill. I passed three women with walking poles; then I crossed paths with a big group of about ten people. This trend continued for some time, and I must have seen at least seven or eight different groups of people out on the trail. They all looked like they were out for a day hike and were not walking the length of the Ridgeway.

The trail was white and chalky, bordered on both sides by lush green grass. The sky was overcast and gray; there was a slight breeze, and the air was delightfully crisp. It was the perfect day for walking. I was so pleased that I had waited until September for my walk, rather than planning it during the summer heat.

I had just finished two courses at the Woodcraft School near Midhurst in West Sussex: an advanced bushcraft course and a wildlife tracking and identification course. It was now apparent to me all the details I could take in that I never noticed before. I found myself bending down to get a closer look at some scat to see if it was deer or sheep. There had been both along the trail so far. I noticed rabbit holes and badger setts and all kinds of other signs of wildlife that I would have previously just passed by without noticing. My walks were now a much richer experience: I was now very much aware that I was passing through a highly-populated area: not by humans, but by animals.

It was a short day on the Ridgeway. I only had eleven miles to walk to reach Wendover that afternoon, where I would be staying at the Red Lion. That meant that I could take it easy on my first day and ease into the trail. It had been ages since I had been out on a walk, and I knew my body wasn't actually in good walking shape. But I had been running, and I had gotten back into my kickboxing classes after lockdown had lifted, and I knew I was in some sort of shape.

The trail turned into a wide, grassy track as I crossed a field. I passed another small group of women walkers just before I went through a gate, then crossed the road to continue along the route. I was already seeing signs for Icknield Way, which follows the Ridgeway for some of its stages, turning off it for others.

I had never heard of the Icknield Way until I walked the Ridgeway the first time. The official route—stretching 170 miles (274 km) from Wiltshire to Norfolk—is relatively new and has been a recognized trail for walkers only since 1992. Twelve years later, it was developed into a multi-use path to make it available for horse riders and cyclists. The modern version of the trail connects the Ridgeway National Trail to the Peddars Way National Trail.

However, the Icknield Way is much older: it's another ancient trackway much like the Ridgeway. Dating back to the

Iron Age, its name is Celto-British, and it's been suggested that it may have been named after the Iceni tribe. The Iceni were an ancient British tribe that lived during the Iron Age and early Roman era in what is now the eastern part of England. The importance of the Icknield Way continues throughout history: it's one of four highways that appear in 12th-century literature, along with Watling Street, Ermine Street, and Fosse Way. The first of these three is another ancient British road; the latter two are Roman roads.

It was the second week in September, and it already felt like autumn. The hawthorns were covered with bright red haws that were a dark burgundy on some trees. The wild roses were adorned with orange-red rose hips. The blackthorns offered up their dark blue-black sloes, perfect for making sloe gin. Elder trees boasted clusters of shiny black berries. Guelder rose bushes were brimming with red berries as their leaves also turned a bright red. The first mushrooms were out, scenting the trail with their woody, earthy fragrance. There was such an air of abundance on the path at this time of the year.

I walked steadily downhill toward Tring. The trail was now woodsy, lined with trees. The walking groups had now subsided, and I only saw the occasional runner or dog walker. There was a bench every once in a while alongside the trail, but I didn't need a rest just yet. Despite the resolution I had made to "rest early and often" when I walked the South Downs Way in September of the previous year, I felt energetic today. I resolved to save my break for when I reached Tring Park.

The Ridgeway came out onto a road, where I turned right. I passed Tring Station, the Grand Union Canal, and the turnoff to Pendley Manor, where I had stayed on my first Ridgeway adventure (and which had since been completely renovated). The trail continued along a quiet country road before turning off once again into a more natural setting. I walked down a fenced-in path, then crossed two A roads.

Great Britain has a road numbering scheme. A-roads are the main roads and are often quite busy. There's an elaborate system for naming them: the roads with single-digit numbers reflect the most important routes coming out of London and are numbered counting clockwise. There are also A-roads with two, three, and four digits—these are sometimes slightly less important roads, but not always.

B-roads are known as "distributor" roads and are low-to-moderate capacity roads designed to move traffic from local streets to arterial roads. They are often smaller and less transited than A-roads, but again, not always.

These designations are important to keep in mind when you're studying your maps for the walking route. It's easy to forget about the danger of cars when you're all alone in the middle of nature. Coming across a fast-paced road can be jarring. But when you've got an A road coming up ahead, you'll need to pay attention and be extra vigilant about crossing. Of course, you'll need to be careful crossing any road—whether it's an A, B, or minor road—but expect fast-moving traffic on the A roads.

I was convinced that Tring Park was just up ahead, but it was not. The trail continued along between fields before crossing another two roads and finally entering the park. Unlike my first Ridgeway journey, when I passed through on a Saturday afternoon in summer when the park was full of people, today it was quiet and peaceful. I continued along until I spotted a large bench through the trees, just off to the right side of the trail. It had been carved with the word "tranquil." That sounded perfect to me.

I settled in for lunch and to rest. I had not yet been walking for two hours, so I didn't bother taking off my shoes. As it was September, and it wasn't meant to rain during the week, I had worn my usual three-season Salomon hiking shoes. They were more lightweight than my leather Scarpa boots and were much better for the warmer months. Hot feet can lead to blistered feet, and that was one thing I wanted to avoid.

I had a leisurely lunch and pulled out my guidebook to peruse this portion of my journey. So far, most of the trail looked familiar to me, even though I was walking it in the opposite direction. After about a half-hour, I stood up to continue my travels through Tring Park.

Tring Park is a 328.5-acre (132.9-hectare) site located to the south of Tring, about halfway between Aylesbury and Hemel Hempstead. The park, much like the Ridgeway, runs along the Chiltern ridge. It sits within the Chilterns Area of Outstanding Natural Beauty. You might see green woodpeckers, great spotted woodpeckers, lesser spotted woodpeckers, red kites, long-eared owls, and kestrels. Nuthatches, chiffchaffs, and willow warblers also live here. The park is also home to field voles and edible dormice (though you probably won't see them). You can also spot such butterflies as the Orange-tip, Peacock, Purple emperor, Ringlet, and Speckled wood (look these up before you go on your journey, so you know what to keep an eye out for).

Before long, the Ridgeway exited the park, turning left on a quiet road called Marlin Hill before turning right onto Church Lane. I passed a few houses as the lane went through the tiny village of Hascoe, then the village hall, then another couple of houses, and I was out of the village and heading into Pavis Wood. As the road was called Church Lane, I expected to see a church, but there was none to be found. I later double-checked my guidebook to see if I had missed it, but I couldn't find it there, either. Once I got home, I checked Google Maps, and it appeared there was no church. Where had it gone?

The path through Pavis Wood was a deep holloway, and the trail had an ancient, magical feel to it. A holloway, or sunken lane, is a path, road, or track that is significantly lower than the land on either side of it. They have usually been formed by hundreds or even thousands of years of foot traffic. They may also have been used to drive cattle in ancient times. Whenever I walk through a holloway, I feel like I'm following the footsteps of Britain's ancient tribes.

There was no one around as I worked my way down the holloway to a quiet road, which I crossed to enter a large field of cows on the other side. All the cows were on the far side of the field, grazing with their calves, and I was able to make my way across it without disturbing them. I'm not afraid of cows, but I'm always on alert when their calves are present—about 5-6 people are killed each year in Britain by cows.

I crossed another quiet country lane. Then the trail passed through another wooded bit before crossing yet another little road and heading into Hale Wood, which flowed into Barn Wood. Forestry work was being done, and I passed a large tractor smoothing out the trail, presumably to get ready for harvesting time—when the logs would be carried out on huge trucks.

The trail started to lead downhill, and I was approaching Wendover a bit earlier than I expected. It was just after two in the afternoon, and I knew that check-in wasn't until three. I decided to sit in the churchyard once I reached it, and rest on a bench until then. I passed a school, then crossed paths with some dog walkers, and finally, I came around a curve in the path and saw the stone wall that encircled the churchyard.

I followed it around, entered through the gateway, and headed straight toward the very same bench where I had rested four years prior. I had wanted to enter the church since I hadn't on my first visit, but it was only open for limited hours due to COVID-19, so I settled in. A handful of raindrops fell and then stopped. I rested for about a half-hour before heading onward into town to find the Red Lion.

I had completely forgotten just how lovely the walk between the church and the town was. It went past twin ponds, and through a pretty little park, before finally heading into the town itself. I turned left onto the High Street and soon found the Red Lion, where I quickly checked in and walked upstairs up to my room for a shower and a rest before dinner.

My room was a small single: semi-refurbished, but spotless. Most importantly, it had a heated towel rack! You may have noticed by now that I get very excited by this simple feature. It makes clothes drying so much easier, especially on a cloudy day. I don't love walking around with all of my clothes hanging off my pack, so a heated towel rack is a much welcome amenity.

Wendover is a fantastic place to stay. It's got everything you need, and more. I had already booked a table for dinner at the Red Lion, but there were plenty of other cafes and restaurants to choose from along the High Street. There's also a Costa for coffee and a reasonably large Budgens for groceries. You'll find a pharmacy, a post office, a WH Smith (should you require any office supplies for your journey), and an ATM just outside the Budgens.

After a quick trip to Budgens for a couple of items, I settled in to write this chapter at the little desk in my room before heading down to dinner. It had been an excellent first day on the Ridgeway. Perfect weather, no pain or blisters, and I felt great. I was looking forward to the challenge of the longer second day on the route: seventeen miles, plus a bit more to get to my accommodation.

The Red Lion is a traditional 16th-century coaching inn, and rumor has it that Oliver Cromwell once stayed here during his rule in the 1600s and addressed his troops from one of the pub's windows. In more recent history, the pub became famous for the 100th birthday of its barmaid, Dolly. She worked at The Red Lion for 75 years, from before World War II until she died in 2015. Dolly was thought to be the world's oldest barmaid.

Dinner at the Red Lion was lovely, outdoors in their small garden. I settled in with a pint of Guinness while I looked over my guidebook for the following day. I wasn't very hungry after having both breakfast and lunch that day, so I opted for a vegetable curry. Unfortunately, as soon as I dug into my meal, I realized that I was, in fact, ravenous, so I found myself forced to order dessert. I was glad that I had had the room for pudding: it ended up being the best sticky toffee pudding I'd had in the entire decade since I moved to the UK.

Back up in my room, I passed the time on my phone as I counted the hours until nine, which I considered an appropriate bedtime. I had spent many nights camping that summer, and I always seemed to be counting the hours to bedtime. At precisely nine o'clock, I turned the lights out, but I suddenly felt wide awake. It was probably all that time on my phone. I was physically tired but energetically ready to get up and go. Not long after midnight, I finally fell asleep.

DAY 2

17.2 MILES (27.5 KM)

After a night of short but quality sleep, I got up at seven with my alarm. I pulled my dry clothes off the heated towel rack and started to pack up my things. I made a cup of tea, forgot about it (yes, this is not a rare occurrence), then rediscovered it just before I went downstairs for an early breakfast.

Rarely do pubs seem to offer breakfast earlier than eight, but the Red Lion starts serving from seven, so I had booked in for 7:30, hoping to get an early start. The waitress was one of those delightful British people who calls everyone "my love," "my dear," and "sweetheart." I know some people find this annoying. I love it. I ordered a full English breakfast, sans black pudding, and settled in to wait. I was starving and ready for a big meal to fuel my long walk that day.

Breakfast arrived within minutes of my order. I ate faster than I would like to admit and found myself checking out of the Red Lion and back on the Ridgeway just after eight. I had a long walk ahead of me—the longest of the week—and I wanted to arrive with enough time to shower before my dinner reservation at seven. I disliked having to book my dinners in advance, but such were the disadvantages of traveling in the age of COVID-19.

I knew I was lucky to be walking a long-distance trail at all this year. My Camino Portugués had been booked for March and had to be canceled, and I never bothered to book the Camino Inglés. While the Camino was now technically open, and Spain and Portugal were accepting travelers, I had no desire to travel internationally. The thought of getting on a flight full of people repelled me.

The sky was clear and sunny, and it was a crisp morning as I walked down the Wendover High Street toward the point where the Ridgeway went back into a more natural setting. I crossed the road and headed up a trail that gently climbed Bacombe Hill.

Bacombe Hill Local Nature Reserve is an area of downland, scrub, and woodland. It was designated a Site of Special Scientific Interest for its chalk grassland. You may see flowers such as wild thyme, clustered bellflower, hoary plantain, pyramidal orchid, bee orchid, and fragrant orchid. The reserve is also a site rich in butterflies: Chalkhill Blue, Brown Argus, Dark Green Fritillary, Duke of Burgundy. Again, look these up before you walk, so you know what you're looking at. I'm much more familiar with plants and flowers than I am with butterflies and birds.

Wildflowers filled the sides of the trail: pale blue pincushion flowers, white yarrow, yellow ragwort. I steadily worked my way up Bacombe Hill and onward to Coombe Hill, where I paused at the monument. The trail now headed alongside the edge of the hill, which was open and sunny, with fantastic views on my right side. There were trees and benches dotted along the edge of the little wood to the left, positioned at regular distances so people could admire the view.

The trail had been quiet so far, with only the occasional dog walker or runner. I passed a dog walker. The man was engrossed in a telephone call, but the dog was instantly interested in me. His ears perked up, and I picked up my pace to move swiftly past them. Not long after, the dog charged at me from behind, barking. I yelped. I could hear the dog's owner apologize from behind me, but I didn't even turn around. I can't stand it when people let their dog off-lead, and then neglect to keep an eye on it.

I clicked on with my poles, passing a small herd of young cows, before going through a gate and into a shady woodland. I soon came out onto a quiet road, which I crossed to enter another wood. The trail was heading steadily downhill, sharpening its incline as it neared another quiet lane. I passed the sign for a farm shop and remembered that this was the point where I had asked the two horse riders for directions on my first journey.

The Ridgeway crossed the little lane to enter Chequers. There were "NO TRESPASSING" signs everywhere. CCTV cameras pointed at the trail as it crossed the entrance to the property. I was still astonished that the trail cut straight through the prime minister's country residence. Despite all the surveillance, it seemed like it would be fairly easy for someone to get quite close to the main buildings—not that I'd want to try it.

I continued through a gate, where I crossed a field to exit the estate. Turning right on the other side of the field, I continued along the border of the property. Trees lined the left side of the trail. Solid metal fencing bordered the field, separating it from the Ridgeway. Someone had written with chalk on three fenceposts: "WORST. PM. EVER." I laughed out loud and stopped to photograph it.

From there, the trail headed downhill to Cadsden, where it crossed a road and passed The Plough pub, with its water tap out front. I was making good time and didn't need water, so I kept going. The Ridgeway now climbed steeply up a hill toward

Whiteleaf Cross. When I was nearly to the top, I saw a rustic bench that had been cut from a fallen tree, so I stopped for a rest.

When I resumed the trail, I went through a gate to enter Whiteleaf Hill Nature Reserve. A poorly excavated round barrow sat to the side of the trail, sadly misshapen. I walked past a car park, which meant there were more walkers out on the trail, then I continued across a road and up Brush Hill. A dog walker was ahead of me, and I crossed paths with another hiker with a big day pack as I went through another gate.

Before too long, I passed a school and knew that I was approaching Princes Risborough, my first milestone of the day. I had mentally broken up the day's journey into sections: first to Princes Risborough, then onto Chinnor, and finally Watlington. I passed New Road, the turnoff to the town, and kept going straight. Now that I was near a town, there were a few more walkers out on the trail, yet the Ridgeway still had a quiet feel.

The route turned off down the pavement of a busier road, and I remembered crossing paths with the runners at this point on my last journey. How hot the afternoon had been that day! I was so grateful that I had decided to no longer walk long-distance trails in the summer. This September afternoon was clear and sunny, but the air felt fresh and comfortable—not stifling and unmanageable.

I passed the Ridgeway Lodge, which might be a great place to stay if you had a car and didn't need to walk into town for dinner. It's located right on the trail. From there, the route went over a level crossing. Once across the tracks, I stepped to the side to allow an older couple to pass with their dogs, but they insisted I go ahead. Just after, I crossed paths with a man who appeared to go across the tracks and onward, in the direction I had come from.

I walked down a tree-lined trail through a golf course then around the edge of a field. As I turned the corner at the field's edge, I saw the same man come up from behind me on the trail. I was surprised to see him again so soon. He greeted me, and I slowed to let him continue onward. I didn't want him walking behind me.

The trail climbed up the steep, chalky Lodge Hill, and I could see the man ahead of me. He paused to rest and look at the view, then downhill in my direction, and then he was soon out of sight. I was still a bit unsettled about how silently and unexpectedly, he had approached me on the trail from behind. I decided I was being silly and stopped at a bench to rest—the same one I had rested upon when I had been suffering the August heat on my previous journey.

My feet were now hot and starting to feel sore. I had been pushing myself that morning and hadn't yet rested my feet. I had been on the trail for three and a half hours at that point, and I became aware that I needed to start taking urgent action to prevent blisters.

After a leisurely rest on the bench—which might once have had a view, but which was now covered with rosebay willowherb and berry-covered brambles—I continued down the shady trail through the little woodland. The path now headed steeply down the other side of Lodge Hill, and I could see a dog walker with four dogs off in the distance. As I caught up to her, I noticed more of them, and a total of about seven off-lead dogs running free. Thankfully, none of them were interested in me, and I passed the woman, who was now walking accompanied by a man and his dog. They were chatting away as I walked on by.

The trail now went into a shady wood, and I passed the sign announcing Chinnor Hill Reserve and barrows, which I had tried unsuccessfully to find on my last journey. I paused, tempted to find the elusive barrow, then continued onward, resolving to return for a day trip to see if I could find the barrows. It now felt like a personal challenge.

When I eventually made a dedicated trip to find them a month later, I realized that I hadn't missed out on anything. They were up high on the hillside and were very eroded. If there hadn't been a sign, I wouldn't have noticed there were any barrows there.

The shady, chalky track sloped gently downwards toward the crossroad that led to Chinnor. Just beyond the road was a bench, where I stopped for another leisurely rest. I found a colorful little painted stone as I sat down: "NHS" read one side, "SMILE" the other. I took a picture of both sides, then returned it to where I had found it.

As I put my socks and shoes back on, I spotted two women not far down the trail who were eying me from a distance. We made eye contact, and I suspected they might be interested in the bench, so I hoisted my pack on my back and headed on. They greeted me as I passed, and when I looked back, they were settling in on the bench. I noticed that one of them had a sizeable Osprey backpack, and I thought they might be walking the Ridgeway. If so, they were the first through-walkers I had seen thus far.

The chalky white track was now fairly level, heading straight ahead toward Watlington and bordered on both sides by greenery. I passed the park where I had rested after my adventure on the Chinnor & Princes Risborough Railway; then the road I had taken down into Chinnor. The second stage of my day's walk was now complete, and I was still feeling good to go. I had made good time thus far, and I was no longer worried about arriving in Watlington for my dinner reservation—I estimated that I would arrive around four, though I had previously worried I might not make it until six. You know me, always worrying about my arrival times.

I passed the deep, water-filled chalk pits that lay to either side of the Ridgeway, which was now bordered by high chain-link fences, which were adorned with numerous signs: "NO

SWIMMING," "NO TRESPASSING," "DANGER," they proclaimed. Every few minutes, I sidled up to the fence to view the deep chalk pits, which had almost vertical sides. Not only that, but they were huge. If a person fell in, it would be tough to get out. I remembered seeing missing dog signs on my first journey, and I could only imagine what had become of them. This was most certainly not a place to let a dog roam off-lead.

After passing all three of the enormous chalk pits, the trail turned into a wide, grassy path, still bordered by trees and bushes. I soon passed the crossroads that marked the turnoff to Kingston Blount, and I knew I was getting closer to my destination. The Ridgeway was still a wide, gentle path that was reasonably flat.

I crossed the A40, then started to hear the noisy M40 up ahead. I passed the Aston Rowant Discovery Trail, spotted the sign for a water tap, which I remembered from my last journey, and paused to read an information sign. A small group of three people and a dog on a lead came down toward the Ridgeway. I almost got tangled up in the dog's lead as it came over to check me out, then I continued on my journey. At least this dog was friendly!

Soon the trail headed down and under the motorway, through a cool, shady tunnel filled with graffiti, some of which had been painted over. The Ridgeway had been almost a straight line since it had come down from Chinnor Hill, and it would continue as such until I reached my turnoff to Watlington.

I passed the crossroads to Lewknor and continued down the very straight, grassy track. I stopped for another rest. Sitting down to the side of the trail, I drank some water and took my shoes off. I could hear a loud tractor off in the distance, which I assumed was working in one of the fields that bordered the trail. As I stood up to resume my journey, I could tell the tractor

was quite close, and I soon saw that it was coming toward me
on the track.

It was fitted with a cutting mechanism and was trimming all
the bushes and brambles that lined the Ridgeway. It made a U-
turn, clipping the left-hand side of the trail as it carried on in
front of me on the track. It was pretty smooth going, so I slowed
my pace and continued behind it. There wasn't much space to
pass it, and I wasn't in a rush.

To my surprise, the man who had overtaken me near
Princes Risborough was now coming toward me on the trail!
We greeted each other, and he carried on past me. What was he
doing? Going back and forth along this portion of the Ridgeway? So far, I had seen him three times today. Thankfully, this
would be the last. I was still unnerved by the fact that I had
seen so much of him.

There was a slight slope up Shirburn Hill, and the track
resumed its level course. I passed one crossroads, then another,
and shortly after, I came to the turnoff to Watlington. I was
tired by this point and gladly walked down Hill Road toward
the village.

I crossed paths with a few people as I headed toward
Watlington, some carrying bags of groceries, others just out for
a walk. I entered the village, turned right down a narrow street,
and found the Fat Fox Inn, where I would be staying once
again. After a short wait, I was shown up to my room, which
was right above the one I had stayed in on my previous trip. It
was spacious and comfortable, with a desk to type up this chapter, and—most importantly—a heated towel rack in the bathroom for my laundry.

It was just after four, which coincided with my updated estimate for the day's journey. I was tired, hot, and aching, and I
welcomed the refreshing shower. It had been a long day's walk.
Laundry done, I settled in to write before heading down for
dinner.

I was ravenous and devoured a plate of fish and chips, along with a pint of Guinness. I followed it up with an Eton mess, then slowly and awkwardly made it back to my room on aching legs to rest before bed. It had been a fantastic day and a great challenge. It was clear that with the right weather, I could walk greater distances—even with a heavy pack on my back. My bag was only a bit lighter than on my first journey: while I was carrying the same number of things with me, I was able to make do with less water.

I was pleased to notice that Watlington had many more shops and restaurants than I had realized on my first visit. Hill Road turns into the High Street, and the area where it crosses paths with the B4009 is the center of the village. Along both roads, you'll find a bakery, a fish and chips shop, another pub, a cafe and deli, a service station, and a Co-op Food. There are many places to stock up on snacks and put together your packed lunch.

DAY 3

14.7 MILES (23.5 KM)

I had set my alarm for eight, thinking it would be nice to sleep in after a long walk. I would be staying at an Airbnb in Goring, and I wouldn't be able to check in until five, so I wasn't in a rush to get back on the Ridgeway. Today was a shorter day's walk by about two and a half miles.

After waking up just after 6:30, I made a cup of tea, forgot about it (do you see a theme here?), then sat down to review the day's journey. I rediscovered the tea just before I went out to the Co-op to pick up some things and drank it. On my return, I went for breakfast, where I chatted about the Ridgeway with the couples sitting at the other two tables. One of them had recently walked the Cotswold Way, and the other was currently walking the Ridgeway, in the usual direction from Avebury to Ivinghoe Beacon.

Breakfast was delivered speedily, unlike on my previous visit. I also learned that the pub was under new management this year, which made a lot of sense. I hadn't been looking forward to returning to the Fat Fox Inn, because service hadn't been so great the first time I stayed there, but I was glad I had. It was an all-around improved experience.

I went back to my room after breakfast and tried to pass the time. I didn't want to leave before ten, but I ended up packing my bag and checking out by quarter-past nine. After a brisk walk up Hill Road, I was back on the Ridgeway. The trail was quiet, and I crossed paths with one woman walking alone and then two women together—locals, probably, out for a morning stroll.

This was the portion of the Ridgeway I had missed on my first journey: I had walked into town via the busy, stressful B480 and had returned down the much quieter Hill Road. This track was a flat, straight stretch of the trail, lined on both sides with trees and bushes. When I reached the crossroads with the busy B480, I was thankful to have discovered a better way to get in and out of Watlington.

Here the Ridgeway continued down a paved road, but the farm offered walkers a more pleasant alternative along the edge of a field, running parallel with the asphalt road. Soon this ended, and I was back on the broad, level track that was typical of many portions of the Ridgeway. I crossed a quiet lane where I saw two walkers and a horse rider, and shortly after, the route turned abruptly left.

More trees were lining the track now, and as it headed uphill, I entered a shady beech woodland. Coming down out of the wood, I crossed another little lane and then stopped for a rest at St Botolphs church. The building itself was closed, of course, but I sat down on the very same bench as I had four years prior. My legs and back still ached from the previous day's long walk, though less than they had the night before. I decided I would be serious about preventing blisters today, and I let my feet breathe.

After a rest, I headed back to the trail, which soon climbed up through a shady woodland before coming out once more onto a wide track. After walking through a farmyard, I crossed one huge field and then another. The last hour or so of the trail had been quiet.

The trail was adorned with brightly colored wildflowers on all sides: blue cranesbill geraniums, pink clover, blue cornflowers, red field poppies, and yellow autumn hawkbit. Occasionally I came across a small patch of mushrooms. I was so pleased that I was walking the trail this time of year: between the abundance of berries and wildflowers, the Ridgeway was full of color.

The route crossed the busy A4130 road and then entered a dreaded golf course, the first of two this day. Unfortunately, here the trail went straight across the green. I looked back and forth as I hurried as fast as I could across it. There were golfers all around, but thankfully none were at the holes that bordered the trail.

Why do many National Trails go straight through golf courses? This seems to be a recurring theme. I imagine that the footpath was there first, before the golf course was designed. Still, it's nerve-wracking to walk straight through the green. Surely I'm not the only one?

I soon came out of the golf course and entered the churchyard of the Holy Trinity Church, which usually offers self-service tea and cake to walkers. Unfortunately, it was closed due to COVID-19, so I sat on a bench to rest, taking off my shoes and socks. This tiny village was Nuffield, the end of the first stage of the day's walk. I was now roughly a third of my way through the day. I was making good time, and it still looked like I would be arriving early in Goring.

After a long rest, I turned left down the little lane and then left again to go up a slight slope into the woods where Grim's Ditch began. This part of the trail had an ancient, magical feel to it. For the next three and a half miles, the Ridgeway ran in a mostly straight line, parallel to the ditch, occasionally crossing over to the other side and then back again.

Grim's Ditch is, as you might imagine, a ditch. This earth-work, dating back to the Iron Age, may have been created to mark territory limits—but archaeologists don't know for sure. It's estimated that Grim's Ditch was built around 300BC. While we don't know what the earthwork was initially named, it was typical for Anglo-Saxons (who date back to 5th-century settle-ment in Britain—several centuries after the ditch was created) to name features of unexplained or mysterious origin "Grim."

This name may come from Wōden (Odin), from the Celtic name Gryn, or from the devil. The latter seems most likely: once Christianity spread throughout Britain, there was a tendency to take place names previously based on pre-Chris-tian deities and re-name them for the devil. You'll find Devil's Dykes and Devil's Punchbowls all across Britain. There are even other Grim's Ditches.

This earthwork is another place—much like Iron Age hill forts—that has an ancient, magical feel. Is it a power spot? Is the energy different here? It certainly feels that way.

After miles of tranquil trail through a narrow strip of wood-land, the Ridgeway came out into the open, where it ran between fields before crossing the bustling A4074 road. It was a bit of a shock to see the elements of our busy modern life after being immersed in the ancient world of Grim's Ditch for over an hour.

Here, the Ridgeway ran parallel to the busy A4130, with only a narrow strip of trees between the path and the road. Before long, the trail turned abruptly left toward North Stoke. As I entered the village of Mongewell, I saw a sign for the church of St John the Baptist, which appeared to be a short detour off the Ridgeway. I followed signs past a series of creepy, abandoned buildings—part of the former Carmel College—to reach the ruined church.

The church of St John the Baptist in Mongewell is no longer open for worship and mostly stands in ruins. It is a Grade II listed building that now falls under the care of the Churches Conservation Trust, a registered charity that looks after redundant churches in Britain. It's estimated that this church dates from the 12th century, though it was remodeled in the late 18th century and restored once again in 1880.

The door was unlocked when I got there, and I was able to go inside. The non-ruined part of the church now consists of a small chancel of Norman origin, with ruined nave walls and a brick tower. The inside is beautifully maintained, with six wooden folding chairs facing the altar. The floor is a beautiful tile mosaic, and there is pretty stained glass in the small windows. It's very tiny but well worth the brief detour it takes to get there. The churchyard is small, dotted with gravestones and yew trees.

By this point, I was tired. I had reached what I considered to be the end of the second stage of my walk, and I wanted another rest—but I was still a bit creeped out by the abandoned buildings I had passed on my way toward the church. I headed back to the Ridgeway, continuing toward North Stoke on tired feet, where I knew I could rest on a bench in the churchyard. I could have done the same at St John's, which was peaceful and pretty, but the whole place had an eerie vibe to it —beyond the creepiness of the abandoned buildings I saw on my approach.

Between Mongewell and North Stoke, the Ridgeway went straight through a golf course, though this time it was along a wide, flat track bordered on both sides by trees. Signs warned walkers: "DO NOT ENTER THE GOLF COURSE—AS YOU ARE AT RISK OF BEING HIT BY A GOLF BALL." It was a shame that the previous one hadn't thought of providing a more sheltered route for walkers, but then the Ridgeway had gone straight across the green.

My tired feet carried me slowly through the pretty little village of North Stoke to the churchyard, where I sat to rest on

—you guessed it—the same bench where I had sat four years prior. I prepared my usual ritual of airing my feet and changing my socks.

By this point, it was very apparent that I would most definitely not be arriving early into Goring. Odds were, I would be right on time for check-in. The walk seemed to be longer than anticipated, but perhaps it was because I was taking more breaks. I always found it deeply puzzling when my estimate for my walking time was so inaccurate—what had I done differently?

I headed out of the village of North Stoke and down a grassy trail that was bordered by a field to my left and the Thames to my right, off in the near distance. The path got closer and closer to the river until it ran right alongside it. Motorboats were out, running up and down along the Thames.

The Ridgeway ran under two massive, double-arched brick viaducts, over which trains rumbled with astonishing frequency. Before too long, I was in the pretty little village of South Stoke and was ready for another break. It seemed like this day would be nothing more than a tour of church benches! I hadn't stopped at this one on my first journey, so I claimed a new bench, one that overlooked the road. Children played in the primary school next to the church and left abruptly after the bell rang at four o'clock. I sat around for a few minutes more, then got up for the final stretch into Goring. I had used Google Maps to calculate the most direct route to my Airbnb, and I estimated I could get there in a half-hour.

Once again, my estimate was wrong, and it took me a full hour. Not long after my five o'clock check-in, I rang the doorbell of my Airbnb, which was no more than a three-minute walk from the Ridgeway. It was the perfect location: close to the trail and close to the village shop and restaurants. My room was a small, immaculate bedroom upstairs. I hurried to shower, wash my clothes, and get ready for dinner at Masoom's.

It was a Friday night, and the place was busy by the time I arrived. I had bumped up my reservation from seven to quarter past six. I wanted to eat, buy my food for the next day, and get back to my room to rest. The food was delicious, even better than I remembered it being. Afterward, I slowly hobbled my way to the Tesco Express and then back to my Airbnb, where I settled in to write this chapter.

I couldn't figure out why I was so tired and achy and why it had taken me so long to reach my destination that day, but after checking my miles on my Fitbit, I saw that I had walked even further than I had the previous day. I couldn't even begin to imagine how I had miscalculated so badly. I only hoped that I had done a better job of estimating the next day's mileage since my accommodation in Wantage was two full miles (3.2 km) off the Ridgeway.

DAY 4

14.8 MILES (23.7 KM)

I woke up just after seven, lay around in bed for a half-hour, then got up and prepared everything. I was out the door just after eight, and in less than five minutes, I was back on the Ridgeway. My Airbnb's location couldn't have been better: not only was it close to the trail, it was close to shops and restaurants as well.

It was a clear day, with a perfectly blue sky full of wispy white cirrus clouds. The morning air was crisp; once again, it was perfect walking weather. I realized that September might be one of the best months for long-distance walking in Britain.

It seemed to take ages to get out of Goring and Streatley, though. First, the Ridgeway ran down a quiet, shady trail between some houses and the river, and then it went through the village of Goring before it crossed the Thames and continued through Streatley. I passed a coffee shop with people inside and considered going in for a hot breakfast, but decided against it: I had another long day ahead of me, and I remembered this being a tedious portion of the trail—long hours of walking, with few attractions to see along it. Today there would be no ancient sites, no churches to visit on the Ridgeway. How I would miss my beloved church benches!

I walked down the pavement through the villages and paused to remove some of the packaging from the food I had bought the night before. My pack was full and heavy, and I wanted to lighten things up, even if it was only by a few grams. I was certainly not an ultralight walker! I tossed some of the wrappers and boxes in a bin and continued onward.

Crossing a busy street, I headed through a residential neighborhood full of huge houses. It was tiring to walk on asphalt for so long, and I had a way to go before I entered a more natural setting. I passed a golf clubhouse and continued until I saw a bench at the side of the road. It awkwardly faced the road, with a house across from it—rather than facing the greenery of a field on the other side of the trail.

Here, I sat down for a mini breakfast. I turned to watch the recently shorn sheep in a nearby field as they trampled all over a stack of wood. A runner approached me and asked if he was still on the Ridgeway. I confirmed that he was, and he carried on.

I didn't sit for long. I got up to continue onward, passing a farm, until finally, the Ridgeway left the asphalt road and gently rose up along a shaded chalky track, lined on both sides by trees. There was a narrow footpath to the left, and I took it. It followed the main trail, but this narrow dirt path was much more comfortable to walk on, and my feet were already tired from an hour of asphalt walking (plus the miles of walking over the previous three days, of course).

Eventually, the little path ended, and I was back on the wide chalky track. I paused to adjust some things in my pack, and a dog walker passed, heading in the same direction as I was. Minutes later, she turned around and headed back down. As we crossed paths, I paused, and we chatted about the trail. She said she had never walked a trail while carrying all her things, and she asked if I would recommend it. I did, very enthusiastically.

The track headed gently down a bit. There were a couple of crossroads, where other byways intersected with the Ridgeway. It now felt very remote, which is very typical of much of the western portion of the trail. Goring and Streatley seemed to be the point that marked the difference between east (Chilterns) and west (open rural tracks) of the Ridgeway.

I saw the occasional walker or cyclist, but there were few people out on the Ridgeway. It was early on a Saturday morning, and the trail was still quiet. I paused for a break at the side of the path, where I took out my leftovers from the night before. I pulled apart the grilled tandoori chicken and dipped it in some hummus that I had bought.

Soon the chicken was gone, and I still had plenty of hummus left. What to do? I looked at the apples I had with me and decided to give it a try. Delicious! I dipped the apples in the hummus and happily crunched away. It was juicy; it was fruity; it was nutty. I had discovered something new.

At one point, I became aware that the apples and hummus honestly weren't delicious together. Instead, they were "outdoors delicious." This is what I call a food, or a combination of foods, that tastes fantastic when you're outdoors: hiking, backpacking, or camping. You're hungry, and just about anything tastes good. This was the case with apples and hummus. It was indeed juicy, fruity, and nutty—but it was not something I would be eating at home.

As I sat, crunching happily away, a small group of walkers passed, then a couple. I must have been resting for quite a while because when I stood up to pull my pack on to get back on the trail, I could see the couple coming back in my direction.

The Ridgeway continued relatively flat and wide, with the

occasional byway criss-crossing over it. I passed over a bridge that carried the trail across a disused rail line, completely overgrown and filled with vegetation. From there, the track came out onto some horse racing gallops, where it turned right to continue down another paved road.

I crossed paths with another couple of walkers, then sat down to the side of the trail for another break. Today, I realized, would be a day of many rest stops. I took my boots off to rest my feet, swapped socks, re-checked my guidebook and maps to see where I was on the trail, and resolved to rest yet again at Bury Down.

The trail continued past never-ending gallops until it went under the busy A34 road—whose tunnel boasted a very detailed mural and poem—before coming up the other side in a shaded, tree-lined area. That didn't last long, as the Ridgeway resumed its wide, chalky track with open views.

I had started to see several cyclists coming toward me. There was a huge cycling event today, and I would continue to see cyclists until I turned off the Ridgeway to head down to Wantage. At least they were coming towards me, rather than from behind. I stopped for another break shortly after the Bury Down car parks. My feet were tired and achy, and I was making good time on the trail and had no need to rush.

The Ridgeway 100 is a 66.5 mile (107 km) cycle race that runs from Chilton to Avebury and back. The cyclists I saw now were approaching the last stage of their race. It was mid-afternoon, and most of them were expected to finish between two and four.

Before getting up, I pulled out a caffeine chew and ate it. I was skeptical as to how much good it would do to ease my tiredness, but between my frequent rest stops and (I think) the caffeine, I felt renewed. I occasionally use caffeine gummies on my longer trail runs, and while I'm not sure whether it's the caffeine that helps or whether it's the placebo effect, they seem to give me energy. I don't drink a lot of it in my daily life—just one long espresso in the morning—so extra caffeine on a long run or hike seems to have an energy-boosting effect.

I continued straight down the broad, grassy track, rutted with the white lines of the chalky trail. The cyclists continued. There were plenty of other walkers and runners on this stage of the route: not only was it a sunny Saturday afternoon, but there were two conveniently located car parks right on the trail.

Not long after, I passed the two small car parks at Cuckhamsley Hill, at the crossroad that led down to East Hendred. I kept looking for another place to stop and rest. I was feeling much better but was in no rush to arrive early. Eventually, I found a good spot in a grassy bit where I could sit alongside the trail, and I greeted the cyclists and walkers who passed by.

From there, the Ridgeway continued in the same form: wide and grassy, lined with chalk ruts. There were expansive views of golden fields to both sides of the trail. This was what I loved so much about the western half of the Ridgeway: the wide views of fields all around.

My experience of this stage of the Ridgeway was so different this time around. No, there were no ancient sites or churches to visit. But it was most certainly not the "tedious" stage that I had remembered from my first journey.

But then I saw a fingerpost sign indicating a place called Scutchamer Knob. Intrigued, I followed the path, which led to a round barrow. Scutchamer Knob, also known as Cuckhamsley Hill, is an Iron Age barrow that has been badly eroded. Upon further research, I learned that this is a much more significant site than it appears. It was initially called Cwichelmeshlaew or Cwichelm's Barrow, and it is recorded as the place where King Edwin of Northumbria killed Cwichelm of Wessex in 636 AD. Later, in the Middle Ages, it became the meeting point of the shire assembly-place. While it was severely damaged by excavation, it would have once been one of the highest points in the area, providing long views across the landscape. It's so easy to pass by this ancient site, but it's worth a quick detour, even if all you see is an eroded mound of earth.

The trail continued straight on until I reached the monument to Lord Wantage, where I stopped to finish my apple and hummus. I was no longer as delighted with this combination as I had been earlier in the day, but it was still acceptable trail food. I only had a quick rest before getting up to go. I was close to the road that marked the turnoff to Wantage, and I felt relieved to be rid of the cyclists. They weren't always good at staying on the other side of the track, no matter how wide it was, and I kept having to hop off into the grassy bits to avoid them.

There were two car parks on either side of the busy B4494 road, and I happily took the footpath down off the Ridgeway toward Wantage. The first two-thirds of the way were grassy trails that sloped gently downhill, and the last bit was along the pavement down a busy road into town. It was smooth going, and I soon arrived at my accommodation for the evening.

I quickly found The Bear Hotel, checked in, and promptly called a taxi service to take me back up to the trail the next morning. I had a short day, and it would be easy to add on another three miles, but there were also three fascinating historical sites along the trail that I was looking forward to spending time at. I didn't want to start my day out with a long uphill slog just to get to the trail.

After a shower, I dressed and walked to the local Sainsburys to get food for the next day. The Rose & Crown, where I would be staying, only served breakfast and Sunday roast, finishing at 3 pm—and I would surely arrive after that. I bought sufficient food for the next day, plus a big bottle of Lucozade, and then I headed back to my room, where I dropped everything off and then walked downstairs for dinner. After a big plate of fish and chips, accompanied by a pint of Guinness, I was ready to settle back into my room for the evening.

DAY 5

8.4 MILES (13.4 KM)

I woke up just before my alarm and was pleased that I had finally been able to sleep in a bit. The heated towel rack had never turned on overnight, and my clothes were still very damp. I tried turning the radiator on again, and it heated up instantly, so I cranked it up high and arranged my laundry neatly across the top.

Worried that breakfast might take too long, I arranged everything else in my pack so that I could be ready to go as soon as possible after eating. I was looking forward to a lovely cooked breakfast, since I knew I wouldn't have a hot dinner upon my arrival that afternoon.

To my disappointment, The Bear was only offering continental breakfast (due to COVID-19), so I contented myself with some watery instant porridge and brown toast with butter and Marmite. I filled up with tea, which was the best part of this sad meal. Thankfully, breakfast was speedy—though not for the reasons I had hoped—and I was back up in my room with plenty of time to get ready before my taxi arrived.

Miraculously, my clothes were now dry, which was the best news all morning. However, my room felt like a sauna, so I quickly turned off the radiator, packed everything up, and checked out early. I waited in the street outside the hotel, where there was a taxi rank. The air was crisp and refreshing, though I knew it would get hot later in the afternoon. Right at nine, my taxi showed up. I hopped in with my pack, and three miles and £12 later, I was deposited precisely where I had left the Ridgeway the afternoon prior.

I hoisted my pack onto my back, crossed the road, and headed off down the wide, chalky track. There had been a couple of people in the car park, but the trail was quiet, and I was all alone—just the way I liked it. The sky was clear, and the air was still crisp, with a slight breeze.

The turnoff to Court Hill Centre—where I had stayed on my first trip—appeared before me, and the Ridgeway veered off to the left, continuing past Whitehouse Farm on my right, then a string of cottages to my left. I crossed the A338 road, which also heads into Wantage, and continued past some houses on my right.

The trail here was a wide, smooth, chalky track. It was blindingly white. I remembered coming down this trail on my first journey and feeling the heat reflecting off the white chalk back onto me. While it wasn't anywhere near as hot this time, it was very sunny, and the reflection was harsh. I never walk or run with sunglasses on, but this is one stage of the Ridgeway where they would be very welcome.

Less than a mile later, I came across the turnoff for Letcombe Castle. This is the largest Iron Age hill fort along the Ridgeway. Fortunately, it's also less known and less accessible than the other hill forts, which means that you'll probably be there all on your own.

This hill fort is so large that a road runs straight through the middle, much like the Avebury stone circle. It's a single track road that leads to a farm just beyond the Ridgeway. Letcombe Castle covers an area of 30 acres (12 hectares) and has an ancient, magical feel to it—as I find most hill forts do. It's dotted with gnarled old hawthorn trees around the rim of the rampart. I was there for about an hour exploring the site, in glorious solitude.

I suspect this hill fort doesn't get many visitors beyond Ridgeway walkers—and even I didn't stop here on my first journey. In fact, I missed the turnoff to Letcombe Castle on my previous trip. It's not very well marked.

Letcombe Castle, also known as Segsbury Camp or Segsbury Castle, has an extensive ditch, ramparts, and four gateways. Excavation suggests that the hill fort was built between 600-700 BC, with regular occupation of the site between the 6th and 2nd centuries BC, when it last appears to have been modified. There is, however, evidence that it was being used around the time of the Roman Conquest in 43AD. It's estimated that it was a communal center for various activities, including sheep management and exchange, which makes sense since this hill fort is larger than the others.

I entered the right-hand side of the hill fort, climbed up on the ridge, and walked all around it. The inner circle was flat and grassy. Deep red haw-covered hawthorns were dotted around the ridge's edge, and I passed them as I circled the hill fort. One of the hawthorns was a wishing tree and had faded, multi-colored ribbons tied on its branches. People had once come here to make their wishes, but that had been years ago.

As I came around 180 degrees on the ridge, the trail sloped down, where I crossed the street and headed up the ridge on the other side to explore the second half of the hill fort. There were views of open farmland all around, patchwork fields of different shades of green and gold. Not a soul was in sight. I was all alone at Letcombe Castle, and it was lovely. I stopped under the shade of a hawthorn to have a morning snack. The watery porridge hadn't been as useful in keeping me fueled as a cooked meal obviously would have.

When I got up to continue, there wasn't much left of the ridge to explore, and I soon found myself on the road, back where I had started. This was such a magical site, and I was reluctant to return to the Ridgeway and continue my journey, though I knew that I could always return to this site—it wasn't too far from home.

The trail was still wide and relatively flat. It was bordered on both sides by grasses and bushes, many of which were still adorned with colorful berries: red-orange rose hips, blue-black sloes, burgundy red haws. Brightly colored spindle shrubs were not only covered with their bright pink fruits, but their leaves were also starting to turn bright red.

There was an alternative walker's path to the side of the trail, but it was so overgrown that it was unusable. I remembered enjoying these side trails on my first journey: the soft dirt paths were more comfortable to walk on than the hard chalk. But this year, every single one that I had seen was so overgrown that it was impassable. I stuck to the firm, chalky track.

From there, the trail sloped gently up Gramp's Hill. More people were out on the trail by now: the occasional dog walker, runner, or cyclist. There were great views all around—patchwork fields dotted with the occasional far-off village.

The Ridgeway climbed a bit more up to Hackpen Hill, where there were once again horse gallops off to my left. I saw the pretty Devil's Punchbowl to the right. I took a narrow footpath through a field to get a better look at it.

There are several sites in Britain—and many more in the United States—called the Devil's Punchbowl. They are usually large, unnatural-looking, bowl-shaped indentations in the earth. Many local British legends tell stories of the devil scooping up giant handfuls of dirt (which causes the punchbowl) and hurling them around.

In Surrey, the Devil's Punchbowl is said to have been caused when the devil threw a handful of dirt at Thor—though another legend about the same punchbowl has the devil being scared by a rooster's crow, leading him to jump into a hiding spot, which caused the massive indentation in the earth. Legend aside, the reality is that these "punchbowls" are often beautiful land formations that are worth looking at, even if you have to take a small detour off the main route.

The track continued past the car park at Sparsholt Firs and went straight on ahead. I paused at the water tap to fill up my bottle. When I had bought the Lucozade the night before, I was thinking I might benefit from some electrolytes, but I wasn't used to the sugary sweetness. I had half left, and when I filled up the rest of the bottle with water, it was the perfect sweetness.

I continued up toward Kingston Hill, where the track sloped down the other side, then back up toward White Horse Hill, where I knew I would be spending some time. It had been full of people when I stopped there on a Wednesday during my first journey, and I feared it would be worse today: a sunny Sunday.

Fortunately, it was not. There were plenty of people, but it wasn't unpleasant, perhaps due to COVID-19. I wasn't used to crowds after so many quiet days on the Ridgeway (except for the cycle event on the previous day), but it was tolerable. I walked around the hill fort to the edge of the hill and sat down with a view of the Manger, Dragon Hill, and the edge of the white horse.

After resting for at least a half-hour, I got up to take some pictures of the view. Then I circled all around the ridge of the hill fort before returning to the Ridgeway. It was a beautiful site with gorgeous views, but it didn't have the same ancient, magical feel that Letcombe Castle did. It probably had something to do with all the people.

From here, the trail was a restricted byway, which is why I was surprised to see a mint green Fiat 500 coming straight up the Ridgeway. Some dog walkers in front of me were indignant and took pictures of the number plate as the car passed. I knew they wouldn't get far, and they didn't, before they had to turn around and pass us once again.

I knew I was close to Ashbury, but I didn't want to arrive much before the 5 pm check-in time. Also, I wanted to spend time at Wayland's Smithy, which I had enjoyed on my first journey. I suspected, however, that it might be full of people. The trail was busy at this point, with hikers coming from both directions.

When I got to the ancient long barrow, it was, of course, packed with people. Children were running around and playing, and adults were picnicking all over. I crossed to the far side of the site and sat down under a beech tree to rest while evaluating my options. I could either wait for everyone to go and have the site to myself or return the following morning.

I decided on the latter. Ashbury was only about a half-mile from the trail, and Wayland's Smithy was only about fifteen minutes from the turnoff to Ashbury. It would be quick and easy to return the next morning.

I sat around a while longer, ate another snack, drank some watery tropical Lucozade (delicious!), and laid down in the leaf litter for a break, my head resting on my shoes as if they were a pillow. Suddenly, I remembered that ticks love leaf litter, and while I had sprayed my trousers with permethrin, I didn't have insect repellent for my skin. I had come down with Lyme disease the previous month, and I did not want to repeat the three weeks of broad-spectrum antibiotics. One was enough. I hurriedly sat up, put on my shoes, and returned to the Ridgeway. I would do a proper check for ticks once I arrived at my destination.

The maps indicate two footpaths to Ashbury, neither of which I took on my first journey. Instead, I had taken the road —which I don't recommend. This time, I consulted the maps:

the first footpath, before the road, headed steeply down to the village. The second, located after the road, looked gentler.

I opted for the first and was so glad that I did. It meandered down a grassy footpath through a sheep field, flanked on both sides by ridged banks. It was gorgeous, and I looked forward to walking up it the following morning. It was like this idyllic country scene out of a nursery rhyme.

Toward the edge of the field was a herd of fuzzy black-and-white belted Galloway cows, along with a pretty black one and five little black calves. I paused to admire them from a distance.

Then I saw the bull. I couldn't remember seeing a "BULL IN FIELD" sign as I went into the field, so this was unexpected. I resumed walking, picked up my pace, and eyed him suspiciously as I went past.

I continued my speedy pace through the next field, glancing behind me every few seconds to see if he was following. The bull was, thankfully, not interested in me. I did, however, decide to reevaluate my plans to return this way on the following morning. Why tempt fate?

Before long, I arrived at the Rose & Crown, where I checked in, showered and did my laundry, lamented the lack of my beloved heated towel rack, then headed back downstairs to write up this chapter in the pub garden. They were not serving food, but there was plenty of time to get a beer.

They didn't have Guinness on tap, only an off-brand stout, which I sadly sipped as I sat out in the pub garden, typing up this chapter and listening to Sinead O'Connor sing "Nothing Compares to You." I agreed: nothing compares to you, Guinness.

DAY 6
9 MILES (14.4 KM)

Once again, I woke up just before my alarm. I felt more or less rested, but everything ached. Recovery seemed to slow down as my journey progressed. Miraculously, half my clothes were dry; I would only have to hang the other half off my pack that day.

Breakfast was quick and satisfying: a full English, with tea. I went down before eight, when I had booked, and my meal was promptly served. I was out the door by about 8:20, heading up the little lane that led past the church. By now, I was used to churches being closed due to COVID-19, so I didn't even pause.

I had considered braving the bull in the field again this morning but decided against it. Plus, by taking the second footpath up to the Ridgeway, I would see something different. This path had a much gentler rise up to the Ridgeway, crossing between fields of grain. This route made for a gentle morning hike, with no livestock in sight.

The morning was already warm, and it was meant to reach 27 degrees this afternoon. I braced myself for a hot, sunny day on the track. I knew what was coming: the wide, open trails of what felt like the true Ridgeway. While this allowed for expansive views all around, it also meant that any walkers, runners, or cyclists were very exposed to the elements.

Arriving at the Ridgeway, I turned left toward Wayland's Smithy, clicking down the trail with my poles. No one else was out, though there were a couple of cars in the parking area where the track crossed paths with the B4000 road that headed into Ashbury. I was so pleased that I had discovered these two footpaths to the village. With two excellent paths leading straight down into Ashbury, I couldn't believe I had taken the road into the village on my first trip. How had I missed these better options? Granted, I wasn't interested in facing the bull again, but yesterday's trail had been gorgeous.

Within minutes I was at the entrance to Wayland's Smithy. There was no one else around, except for a flock of pheasants that scurried away as I entered the site. I took some photos, then walked up the steps on the near side of the long barrow and hopped down into the chambers.

I sat quietly in the middle chamber for several minutes before moving to each of the side chambers. They smelled much like West Kennet Long Barrow: damp and earthy. Hearing voices, I peeked my head up out of the chambers and saw two women walking down the access path. I hopped up out of the chamber and sat on a log. I trusted they wouldn't be long, and they weren't. After taking some photos, they left.

Returning to the long barrow, I sat once again in the center chamber with my eyes closed. I breathed in the earthy scent of the chambers and listened to the robins singing in the trees. I felt deeply relaxed and could have stayed much longer, but the day was getting on, and I had already added onto what was meant to be a short nine-mile day.

Reluctantly climbing out of the chambers, I resolved to return more often to this site. Perhaps I wouldn't come back as often as I had to Avebury, but I didn't want to let another four years go by before coming back. It had a special feel to it, not quite like West Kennet Long Barrow, but different. It was well worth revisiting.

I went back down the way I had come that morning, eventually passing the place where I had come up onto the Ridgeway. Continuing onward, I passed a water tap and paused to fill up my water bladder and top up my bottle. I had departed with one liter in my reservoir and another in my bottle, but I was worried about the hot day ahead.

By now, I was already seeing the occasional dog walker or cyclist. It was a quiet Monday morning on the trail, and this would mark the ambiance for the rest of the day. I would mostly be on my own, crossing paths with very few people. It was a break from the busyness of the weekend when so many other people were out. I was thrilled to be able to enjoy one of my favorite stages of the Ridgeway in solitude.

The track was wide and level and made for easy going. I passed the creepy caravan that I remembered from my first journey. It was no longer adorned with the multitude of flags, as it had been four years prior. There were signs outside, imploring people to pick up their dog mess. A dog bowl with water sat outside the door. Other than that, it looked as if its occupant was not home.

I carried on, passing turnoffs to Bishopstone on my right. I had crossed paths with a couple of Ridgeway walkers and assumed they must have stayed the night in Bishopstone. I enjoyed walking in the opposite direction from the general Ridgeway "traffic," if you could call it that. If the year 2016 had been a quiet year for through-walkers on the Ridgeway, then 2020 was even more so, for obvious reasons (COVID-19). Still, I was thrilled that I had decided to revisit the trail this year rather than wait for the following spring as I had initially intended. It was so beautiful in autumn.

Walking a long trail such as this gave me great joy. I resolved to plan two of them for 2021: one where I would carry my gear and perhaps one where I would stay in B&Bs as I had been accustomed to doing. Perhaps I could plan a journey in April before the heat, and a second in September, which was proving to be an excellent month for walking.

The Ridgeway headed gently up and then down Charlbury Hill, and before I knew it, I could see the car park of Fox Hill in the near distance. I came down the stony track, arrived at The Burj restaurant where I had refilled my water supplies on my first journey, and carried straight on. From here, I would be following a series of busy roads until I reached the turnoff that led up to Liddington Castle.

I headed straight down the road, crossed the busy M4 via a bridge with an all-too-narrow pavement for walkers, and carried on, crossing to the other side of the road as I knew I would be turning left eventually. The Ridgeway turned onto the relatively quiet B4192, where they were doing road works. I walked down the grassy verge, then crossed over to take the trail up the hill toward Liddington Castle.

The route rose gently uphill, with a large field to my left. I passed a pillbox off to my right and paused. I remembered it being much closer to the trail the last time I had passed through, but surely it was in the same place. It felt very disorienting, and I realized how different the path could look when viewed from the opposite direction.

A pillbox is a brick and concrete guard post, usually equipped with holes through which weapons could be fired. In 1940, about 28,000 pillboxes and other field fortifications were constructed in England as part of the anti-invasion preparations of World War II. Only about one-quarter of these structures still survive—some intact, some crumbling to pieces.

Heading steadily up the hill, I took the turnoff to Liddington Castle, turning right to follow the permissive footpath around the edge of the field, then through a gate, turning left to continue up toward the hill fort. I crossed paths with a couple who informed me of a good resting place up at the trig point. I knew that spot very well, and I had been planning for another rest there. I thanked them and continued on.

I went through another gate as I neared the hill fort, then approached the outer ridge, following a narrow trail down into the ditch and up the other side. Reaching the top of the inner rampart, I sat down next to the trig point and took off my shoes and socks. I pulled out my bag of food to have the last of my apples and cheese. The cheese probably wouldn't last another day without refrigeration, and it was debatable as to whether I should even be eating it at this point. It was delicious, though— and not just "outdoors delicious."

Once I felt rested, I took a clockwise walk around the inner ridge of the hill fort. To one side, there were gorgeous views of rolling hills; to the other, Swindon. As I approached the beginning of my circle, I saw a couple coming toward me. We reached the trig point at the same moment, greeting each other. I continued back to the Ridgeway in solitude, backtracking along the permissive footpath that clung to the edge of the field.

From here, I headed ever so slightly downhill along one of my favorite stretches of the Ridgeway. Golden fields were bordering the track, with a patchwork of various shades of gold and green further off. I had left the view of Swindon behind me and could see nothing but rolling hills all around.

I paused again and again to take photos of the trail. The sun was in my face, so I needed to take pictures facing the opposite way. It was compulsive; I couldn't stop: it was so lovely that I wanted to capture it all. These expansive views brought such joy.

There was a shady bench further on where I planned to rest. It was a hot, sunny afternoon, I had only a short walk that day, and I didn't want to arrive too early at my destination. A smaller bench that I didn't remember appeared suddenly before me, and I took a quick break. I didn't take my shoes off; I just rested and enjoyed the view.

An inverted red-on-black ladybug alighted on my left knee, then flew away, only to return. When it flew off once again, I got up to continue my journey, taking photos all along the way. As I approached the little beech wood to my left, I could see something strange and blue next to one of the trees. When I walked past, I saw that it was a collapsed tent with a log on top of it. A cyclist was sitting on the bench, talking on the phone—though he seemed to be unrelated to the tent. I headed to some logs further on, where I knew I could rest as I waited for him to leave.

This time, I took off my shoes and socks for a real rest. I could see one of his handlebars just beyond a tree, and the gentle breeze brought me the faint murmur of his voice, so I knew he was still there. I waited. The second couple I had seen at Liddington Castle passed by, and we greeted each other. Eventually, I became aware that my feet were ready to go, and so I did—even though the cyclist continued on the bench.

I passed a crossroads, heading to Lower Upham Farm to my right, with Upper Upham to my left. I laughed to myself about the silly place names and continued. The day was still hot and sunny, with not a cloud in the sky. I reflected on how British weather has such a bad reputation, yet I never seemed to have rain when I walked these trails. I would have welcomed a bit of cloud cover on a day like this. British weather is truly unappreciated—at least during the warmer three-fourths of the year. Winter always seemed to bring an abundance of mud.

Reaching a shadier bit, I saw what appeared to be one of the narrow alternative footpaths off to the right. Again, it was too overgrown to even consider attempting—what a contrast to my first journey, when it had been better maintained. Its shade would have been welcome.

I crossed another road, this one heading to the abandoned

village of Snap, and continued straight on. Again, there was an overgrown footpath to my right. I ignored it. A huge tractor rumbled past at what felt like top speed, and I hopped off into the grassy verge to avoid it.

There were open fields to both sides, and I could see to my right the high ridge that I would be walking on the next day, my last on the Ridgeway. I was disappointed that my journey would be over so soon. Just one more day, and a short one at that. And then Avebury, my final destination.

I had been debating where to depart the trail for Ogbourne St George. There were several options, but it was only three, and check-in wasn't until four. I passed the first turnoff, which headed steeply downhill toward the village. I knew this trail and did not relish the idea of walking up it first thing in the morning, so I carried on.

The Ridgeway veered off to the right, and I stopped in a shady, grassy bit for a final rest. Taking my shoes off, I drank some water and once more evaluated my options. I could continue on the Ridgeway, around Ogbourne St George, and through Hallam—or I could take the turnoff right in front of me. I checked the time and decided to continue. Departing the trail here would also mean a hike uphill the next morning, much like the previous turnoff. If I continued through Hallam, I knew there wouldn't be much of an ascent the next day. I was thankful that I understood how to read the contour lines on the OS Map—otherwise, I would have started the morning's walk with a steep ascent.

The route was now a gorgeous shady trail, lined on both sides by lush trees and greenery. The rosebay willowherb plants had all gone to seed and were adorned with fluffy white tufts of wool. Heading gently downhill toward the busy A346 road, I passed the water tap outside Elm Tree Cottage and paused. I was so close to my destination that I decided to carry on. It felt a bit strange to walk straight up to the house to use their tap, even though it was sign-marked both on the house and in my guidebook.

The A346 was tricky to cross, but I didn't have to wait too long. I quickly passed through the tiny village—hamlet, perhaps?—of Hallam, then turned right at the footpath that would take me into Ogbourne St George. I headed gently downhill through grassy fields. My body was tired and stiff, and going up and over the stiles was a bit of a challenge. I realized how fortunate I had been that the Ridgeway itself was free of stiles.

The footpath veered off to the right, went over a little bridge, then veered slightly right once more before heading straight down the edge of the field and into the village. I turned right and headed straight to the Inn with the Well, which was open.

I was shown straight to my room, which was thankfully at the far end of the building, away from the pub's outdoor seating. They had converted much of their car park into an outdoor dining area, with white garden tents shading people from the hot sunshine.

After a cool shower and some hot tea and biscuits, I relaxed in my room. There was, as I had expected, a heated towel rack for my laundry. The two hours between my arrival and my dinner reservation passed quickly, and I headed to the pub, ravenous despite my numerous snacks that afternoon.

"You looked so cool when you arrived," said the inn's owner as she poured my pint. "Everyone else looked so frazzled." I was surprised to hear her words since I had felt so hot and tired by the time I arrived earlier that afternoon. Yet I knew that the final rest stop I had taken where the Ridgeway sloped down on the approach into Ogbourne St George had helped me to arrive in good shape. I had taken the long way into the village, setting me up for a good departure the following morning.

This was my third time staying at The Inn with the Well—

once on my first Ridgeway journey, the second time earlier this year when I was camping and walking before the first lockdown happened, and now. Not only did they give me a 10% discount for booking directly with them, but my pint was on the house. I settled in to write this chapter, sipping my Guinness and waiting for my double cheeseburger and fries. Pub food is always satisfying after a long walk.

DAY 7

10.2 MILES (16.3 KM)

After waking up ridiculously early, I went back to sleep, tossed and turned for a bit, and woke up with my alarm, which felt like an outstanding achievement. I had finally slept just a bit more than eight hours, which should be easy to accomplish, considering how exhausted I was at the end of each day. It was very apparent just how hard it was to get a good night's sleep each night when changing location every single day.

I had a fantastic cooked breakfast inside the pub, with everyone I had seen at dinner the night before sitting at their assigned tables. We all chatted a bit about the Ridgeway and other trails. One of them was another Ridgeway walker, and he gave me some ideas for new adventures. I always found it useful to hear firsthand stories from other hikers—you can only learn so much from a guidebook. That's why I find books about long-distance trails to be so useful —I initially chose the Ridgeway because I read Andrew Bowden's book on it.

After a satisfying meal, I headed back to my room, packed everything up, and was on the trail just after 8:30. I walked down the High Street, then back up the gentle grassy fields toward the Ridgeway. Once on the trail, I crossed paths with a young woman who appeared to be still in her pajamas, out for a morning stroll.

The sky was clear and sunny, with a slight haze off in the distance. A light breeze freshened the morning air, but I could tell it was going to be hot again. The refreshing crispness to the air that I had started with on my first couple of days of the Ridgeway was now gone. Summer had returned.

The trail curved around the village, then turned left to head back onto the ridge. The first bit was shady and wooded, and I crossed paths with two women who were walking the western half of the Ridgeway—except they were wild camping along the way. We chatted for a bit. I wanted to walk a trail like the Ridgeway, but camping rather than staying in B&Bs, so I asked them what it was like.

As I suspected, I would have to dial back my daily miles when carrying such a heavy pack. With my small, 36-liter bag, I had gone from an average of 12 miles each day on my first journey to the longer 17-mile days I had managed on this one. I knew that my hiking fitness was improving, but I also knew that would change once I attempted my first long-distance trail with a bigger, heavier pack. We wished each other a good journey, and each continued on our own way.

The trail headed slowly uphill, now open and exposed, running between fields. I passed a fenced-in reservoir on my left and continued, past a herd of disinterested cows. From there, I climbed steadily up to Smeathe's Ridge, with views of farmland all to my right and horse gallops to my left. I paused to watch four dark horses charging up the hillside, then coming down again. Morning exercises?

It was a quiet Tuesday morning on the Ridgeway, with very few people out on the trail. I crossed paths with two cyclists, the first people I had seen in some time. The grassy track headed gently down the other side of the hill, crossed a quiet country lane, and abruptly entered the Barbury Castle Country Park. I was not ready for this landmark, which I knew was reasonably close to Avebury—the day was already going by too quickly.

Not only was I advancing faster than I expected, but the site was full of people. Perhaps "full" is not the appropriate word. There were a man and an older woman, two young women with a baby, a young couple, a man on his own, sitting on the far side of the hill fort, and a few others. But it was always shocking to see more than a couple of people in one place after the quietness of the trail and the craziness of the 2020 lockdown.

After wandering around the (closed) toilet blocks looking for a water tap (there was none), I walked into the center of the hill fort and sat down for a rest. I took off my shoes and relaxed. A buzzing sound approached before long, and I looked up to see a drone heading toward me. I shaded my eyes with my arm to look up at it, and it paused, hovered above me, then returned from where it had come. After that, it buzzed back and forth across the hill fort before finally disappearing altogether.

Once I was ready to get going, I hoisted my pack back onto my shoulders and headed up the inner ridge of the hill fort. Unlike the others I had visited this week, Barbury Castle had not one, but two, ridges or ramparts. I walked a full circle around the inner ridge, considered doing the same around the outer rampart, and decided against it. I craved the remoteness of the Ridgeway, and so I headed straight down through the middle of the hill fort, where the trail passed through it.

On the other side, I passed a quiet road and headed straight down the wide chalky track. I crossed paths with a lone walker. There were more horse gallops off to my left and patchwork fields to my right. The trail here was mostly level, heading in a straight line along the ridge.

Less than an hour after I had left Barbury Castle, I came across a small plantation of trees that I had visited before. The day was now hot, and I wanted to rest again—this time, in the shade. I entered through the small gate and walked a circle around the little beech grove before finding a spot next to a tree. I pulled off my shoes and socks and dug into my food bag for a snack.

A couple of walkers passed by the grove as I rested; I could see them from my spot where I rested against the large beech. When I was ready to go, I swapped my socks, picked up my bag, and headed back onto the trail. In just a few meters, I passed the car park at Hackpen Hill. I crossed a road, took a slight detour off the trail toward the white horse that was carved into the side of the hill, then turned around when I realized it was best viewed from afar. I'm not sure what I was expecting—I know how hard it is to appreciate the white horses from the same hill they've been carved into.

The chalky trail sloped gently downward, still heading in a straight line. Before long, it became more of a stony track, which was a bit uncomfortable to walk on. There were grassy bits on both sides of the trail, and I walked on those when I could. Now there was a bit of shade from the trees and bushes on both sides of the track.

Less than a half-hour after my rest in the shady beech grove, I came across a massive log and stopped for another rest. The day was hot, my feet ached, and I was in no rush to arrive at Overton Hill. For one thing, I was unable to check in before 4:30 that afternoon, and for another, I didn't want the journey to end. It was always so sad to end a long-distance trail.

A couple of walkers passed by as I rested, and just a few minutes later headed back in the other direction. I swapped my socks yet again, got up, and continued my journey. Not long after, I saw a comfortable bench, beckoning to me from its location in the full sun. Perhaps it would be a good spot on a cloudy day, but not on this sunny afternoon. How I was taking for granted this warm, sunny day! I would long for it the following winter when the trails turned to mud.

I was now very familiar with this portion of the trail, having revisited it on my many trips to Avebury. I passed Fyfield Down to my left, with its gray sarsen stones dotted throughout it. There was the occasional sarsen alongside the track.

Fyfield Down is part of the Marlborough Downs and is located about 1.5 miles (2.4 km) north of Fyfield village, near the town of Marlborough. The down is a Site of Special Scientific Interest and has the best natural collection of sarsen stones in all of England, known as the Grey Wethers (and are marked as such on the OS Maps). If you've got the time and energy, the fields of sarsen stones make for a good detour from the Ridgeway. I had been here before, and so I continued onward.

The Ridgeway followed its straight course along the ridge toward Overton Hill. It was once again chalky and, in some places, was deeply rutted. I was all alone on the trail and had been for most of the journey since Barbury Castle. I crossed the byway that led down to Green Street in Avebury and paused. I was now very close to the end of the trail and that end-of-trail sadness began to loom up before me like a dark cloud. I was in very familiar territory, as I had walked this route many times on trips to Avebury. Green Street is part of the Avebury circular walk recommended in my guidebook.

The wide track now sloped ever so gently downhill. In a desperate attempt to stretch out the journey, I had one final rest to the side of the trail, in a soft, grassy bit. It had probably not been much more than a half-hour since my previous rest, but I didn't care. I wanted to drag this journey out as long as possible. I snacked on some nuts and greeted a solo cyclist as he passed. Then I swapped my socks and stood up for the final stretch toward Overton Hill.

To the far right, I could see just the tip of Silbury Hill off in the distance. There was a tumulus in the field to the left of the track, and further on, I could see the three tumuli that sat near the western terminus of the Ridgeway. To the right was the car park at Overton Hill. My heart sunk. I was even closer than I had thought.

In just a few minutes, I reached the end of the trail. I felt gutted that it was over so soon, but that is the nature of walking a long-distance trail—it has to end sometime. I took some photos with the Ridgeway signs, then crossed the busy A4 road to the Sanctuary, which I circled before heading down the steep footpath toward East Kennett. The trail curved gently to the right, passed over a small bridge that carried the path over the now-dry River Kennet, and then opened up onto a paved road in the middle of East Kennett.

I stopped to give directions to a couple who were looking for the West Kennet Long Barrow, then I turned down a narrow footpath and headed toward the church, which I knew would be closed. I was hoping for a quiet bench to rest on, but this was the first churchyard I had ever seen without a bench. Luckily, there was one on the side of the road that approached the church. I passed it as I went to The Old Forge to try and check in early.

There was no answer, so I returned to the bench and decided to wait for a half-hour before trying again. It seemed the entire village was out. The woman who lived in the house opposite drove up and entered her property, closing the gate behind her. A man passed and commented that I had found the "village bench" (indeed, I had—it was hard to miss). A couple more cars drove past me on the narrow street, and the local bus dropped off two schoolgirls, who greeted me as they passed.

When the half-hour was up, I returned to The Old Forge and tried again. Thankfully, the owner was there, and I was able to enter my room. I showered, rested, drank plenty of liquids, and settled in to write this chapter as I munched on some nuts in my spacious room. This was another night without a hot dinner—all of the local pubs were closed.

This 2020 Ridgeway experience had been so much easier than my previous one in 2016. Yes, my feet and legs ached—and sometimes my back and shoulders, too. But I had put in longer days, and I had been just fine. And, perhaps best of all, I had done so blister-free. It was possible!

I was already contemplating my next walk. When could I fit it in? Could there be another one before the year's end? Was that too much to ask for? I couldn't wait to start researching my options.

Sadly, another 2020 walk was not to be had, as the UK entered lockdown yet again as the year progressed. But I had high hopes for the new year— when I might finally walk the Dales Way, which I had wanted to hike for several years. I might even camp rather than stay in B&Bs!

AVEBURY

I woke with my alarm, then gathered my things together and went into the main house for breakfast. While I had stayed in a private room within the house on my first stay, this time, I had been placed in a large self-contained room that had its own external entrance. I had more privacy, and a small kitchenette as well.

Sitting down at the big table, I waited for breakfast. I was greeted and served by the hostess. There was no sign of the husband or daughter who had attended me on my first visit.

I ate quickly, then went back to my room, packed the final items into my bag, and was off for a day around Avebury. First stop: West Kennet Long Barrow. I walked down familiar paths between East Kennett and the ancient monument. It was a quiet morning, with no one else out.

The crossroads to the long barrow soon appeared before me, with the large old oak to the right of the path. I turned left, walking up the gentle slope to the top of the hill where the barrow sat. No one was around.

I went up to the site, paused at the stony entrance, then went inside. I did my usual check inside each of the five chambers to reconfirm that I was alone, then I set my pack down in the largest chamber at the end. The long barrow was full of "ritual rubbish"—used tealights, dripping candle wax, and all kinds of other things that people had left in the site after their rituals. Ritual rubbish is a huge pet peeve for me and others. I remember reading in Peter Knight's book about West Kennet Long Barrow how he would regularly visit the site to remove the trash. I knew that I wasn't the only one to clean these things up; I had visited the long barrow many times before, often in the evening on one day and then again the following morning —and items I had seen in the evening had been cleaned up before my visit the next day.

I now pulled out a small plastic bag to do my cleanup. I walked through the site, first gathering all organic rubbish, and carrying it outside. Then I popped all the used tealight tins into my bag, peeling the melted candle wax off the ancient stones and adding it to the bag. There were photographs, too, though I left those where they sat.

Many people don't think about the impact of their actions. Either that, or they don't care. But it's disrespectful to leave these things at a sacred site. The organic items are easy enough to clear, but there's no excuse for the tealight tins and the melted wax.

The concept of "leave no trace" applies not just to hikers and campers but to those who hold rituals in these sacred sites. It is perfectly reasonable to bring flowers, crystals, and candles into places like this, but it's essential to take these things out with us when we finish the ceremony. Clearing up our ritual items shows respect for the place and future visitors. Leaving them there is a great disrespect for the site and other visitors.

Rubbish cleared, I settled down in the big chamber to soak in the energy of the site. I stayed for about an hour, then began to feel unsettled. It was getting on in the morning, and there would soon be other visitors. I placed my plastic bag, now full of rubbish, into the top of my pack and exited the long barrow.

As I walked down the hill, I could see cars arriving in the layby. People were already beginning to come uphill to the site. I had left just in time to avoid them.

We greeted each other as we crossed paths, then I directed my journey toward the sacred spring nearby. Arriving at the site, I climbed over the fence, crossed the river, and dropped my pack at the other side. This spring is another place I know well, having visited it many times before, in all seasons.

An old willow arches over the site and is adorned with multicolored ribbons. This is another place of sacred worship. There are letters to loved ones who have passed and other memorials. The wishing tree is filled with hanging baubles and strips of fabric. Thankfully, there is no spilled candle wax or empty tealight tins.

Avebury is a place where you will find many wishing trees. This is a long and ancient custom in Britain. Traditionally, people would tie a strip of fabric torn from their clothing to a tree or bush situated near a sacred well. This would be a natural fabric, such as cotton or linen, and it would biodegrade over time.

In tying a clootie (a wishing ribbon), people would make a prayer to the guardian spirit of the well or spring, which was often connected with healing. The idea was that as the strip of fabric degraded over time, the person's symptoms or illness would lessen. When the cloth had disintegrated entirely, they would be cured.

Unfortunately, that is no longer the case when we use modern day ribbons, which are usually made of synthetic materials, and I will continue here on my leave no trace rant. If you must leave something on a wishing tree or clootie well, please use only biodegradable fabric (you can buy 100% cotton ribbons online). You could also use a thin cotton thread. It is generally recommended that you not tie the ribbon on, but rather drape it over the branch of the tree or bush. If you do tie the ribbon on, make sure it's loose enough that the plant has room to grow.

I settled down next to the willow to soak up the energy of the place. If you've read my book *If Trees Could Talk*, you may be familiar with this site. The willow did not appear as one of the 28 trees featured there, but it now expressed interest in sharing a story for my next book about trees. I pulled out my phone to channel its message.

I was pleased that this tree—which was so special to me— had chosen to participate in my new tree project. I had the feeling that it might make an appearance in my first book on trees, but it did not. Now I understood that it had been saving its story for the second one.

Before long I felt that it was time to move on, and so I did, walking toward Avebury and taking a detour to visit Windmill Hill, another of my favorite Avebury sites. Windmill Hill is not a hill fort, though you might mistake it for one. It is a Neolithic 'causewayed enclosure', with three concentric ditches, rather than ramparts, as a hill fort would have. It forms part of the Avebury World Heritage Site, and is located just 1.5 miles (2.4 km) from the stone circle.

Several trees from my If Trees Could Talk book are located at the little wood at the top of Windmill Hill, and I went straight there to visit them. As always, I went first to the big sycamore, where I took off my pack, set it on the ground, and climbed inside its clustered trunks. I chatted with him for a while, giving him an update on how the book was doing. I told him about the new book, and then I rested among his trunks for some time.

This day was beginning to feel like a reunion with my beloved trees. From there I moved to visit The Three Witches, then The Four Knights, also located within the little wood. And then it felt like time to move on, so I put on my pack, said good-bye, and headed through the site and down toward the Avebury stone circle.

I was still adapting to being around larger groups of people, and of course the stone circle was much busier than any of the other sites I had visited so far this morning. It's always a rough adjustment between the quiet of a long-distance trail and the noise of everyday life. Avebury is a good transition point, as it's full of people yet it's quite a large site.

After walking around the four quadrants of the stone circle, I settled in to have lunch on a picnic table near the barn museum. I was meeting my husband here, and we would drive back home together. I had planned a route for him to run around Avebury, and he would come and find me once he was finished. In the meantime, I would wait in this slightly sheltered spot.

I was still feeling post-trail sadness, and I grieved the end of my journey as I waited. Reflecting on my trip, I was grateful that I had decided to walk the trail in the opposite direction. It was so much more meaningful to end the route in Avebury rather than to start it here. I wondered why the guidebooks always recommended the opposite direction, from west to east.

By the time my husband finished his trail run and met up with me, I was (emotionally) ready to depart for home. Much like my second South Downs Way adventure, my second Ridgeway walk was so much more delightful than the first time around. Each journey truly was distinct, even though it was along the same route.

I was different. My perspective was different. And my story was different.

EPILOGUE

This second Ridgeway adventure lived up to my expectations for it—and then some. I'm so happy that I revisited the trail. I know some people who say they'll never re-walk the same route again, but I can't say that for myself. It's a different adventure each time. And because I'm a more experienced long-distance walker, I've tweaked a lot of the details that plagued my first journeys with aches and pains.

However, long-distance walks can be a great space for healing. I often find that my fears and limiting beliefs will arise during the journey. It's like my mind pulls them up to the surface of my awareness so I can work on—and heal—them. This is one of the reasons why I love solo walks: it's just me and my thoughts—for better or for worse.

As I usually do on my long-distance routes, I pulled one oracle card for each day of my journey, plus an extra card to represent the overarching theme of the trip. Below, I share a little more of my inner experience of walking the Ridgeway the second time around.

Wild yam: intuition, omens, femininity

On my first day of the journey, it was like a fear was triggered that played its way out over the next couple of days of my journey. I am not normally paranoid when I walk, and I make a big deal about how important it is for me to journey alone on these trails. Sometimes I get fearful if I see a person acting strangely, but it doesn't happen too often. However, this Ridgeway walk brought up some unpleasant fears.

This first day I was walking with my phone in airplane mode—which was customary for me— to save the battery. I disabled it at one point to share a picture on Instagram and saw an alarming number of texts from my husband saying: "My messages aren't being received. What is going on? What is wrong? Is your phone turned off? Is everything okay?" I replied, "Oh no, I always walk with my phone in airplane mode, you know that." And his response was, "From now on, please don't."

I stopped walking with my phone in airplane mode, which isn't even necessary because I always carry an extra power bank with me in case of emergency. I did not bring my solar panels with me on this trip, but I have done so on previous adventures.

There was something about his message that triggered this fear that carried on into the next couple of days. It was like an omen: because I'm a woman, I'm in danger. Of course, injuries and accidents can happen to anyone on a long-distance trail, but that's how my fearful mind interpreted it. It's key that a friend or family member be able to locate you through your phone when you're out on a route like this; otherwise, it might be difficult to find you in case of an emergency.

Multiflora rose: antagonism, conflict, disharmony

The next day of the walk was from Wendover to Watlington, which was where I was walking down the trail and crossed paths with this random male walker. About ten minutes later, I realized that he must have turned around just after he crossed paths with me. He came up behind me (quite silently), then passed me and went up the hill.

I talked a bit about this in the main part of this book, but I tried to make light of it. In reality, it was something that occupied my mind the entire day. Seeing him three times throughout that day was really unsettling. All I could think was, "Why did he turn around?" At first, I thought, "Maybe he turned around to go to his car." But of course, that wasn't it, which I realized when I saw him the third time, near the end of the day.

I was already on edge from the previous day's ominous message, and seeing this man so many times brought up all of this paranoia inside me. Throughout the entire day, I felt all this conflict and disharmony and fear—just like the oracle card said. And that was what my mind was working through this entire day.

I was on hyper-alert all day because of this man. I didn't see him for several hours on the trail, and then about a half-hour before I arrived at my destination that evening, I saw him again, walking towards me. It appeared that he had walked all the way to somewhere past me and then turned around to come back again.

Logically, he was probably just having a day walk where he was walking back and forth along the Ridgeway, but it triggered a lot of fear and caused it to bubble up to the surface of my consciousness.

Oak: wisdom, masculinity, strength

Day 3 was the day where I was thinking about this man from the moment I stepped back on the trail. What would I do if I saw him again? The fear was still very present, but I had reviewed my daily theme before leaving my accommodation, and I was aware that it was "wisdom, masculinity, strength."

As I had in the past, I began using this as a kind of a mantra. I was walking along thinking: "Wisdom, masculinity, strength. Wisdom, masculinity, strength." Every time my mind would go to fear, I would go over this mantra in my head and force myself to think: "Men aren't always scary. They can represent wisdom and strength, and good things."

This day was very much about overcoming my fears. I finally calmed down that afternoon and had a lovely walk at the end—once I realized that the guy was nowhere in sight or anywhere on the trail in the segment that I was walking.

Plantain: innocence, naiveté, unaware

This was a Saturday, and there were so many people out on the trail that it calmed my fears. This was also the day of the cycle event, where I kept crossing paths with all the cyclists. It was so lovely to see all these people out on this ultra-challenge, and I was feeling so proud of them. I had seen so many that I felt some kind of solidarity with these guys.

Then, at the end of the trail, when I got to the turnoff to the town where I was staying, I heard this cyclist get hit by a car. I didn't include this in the actual book chapter for this day because it was such a huge shock to me. But it was like I was just ambling along in this naive innocence, and then boom.

I went to try and help, but there were already people attending to him, and they had phoned emergency services, so there wasn't anything to do. I ended up walking straight to where I was staying that night and kind of collapsing in a chair in my room. I didn't actually see the accident, but it was very unsettling. It just knocked me off my balance.

I was finally getting back to my center after being paranoid about the walker, and then this really knocked me off-balance. I think this card represented that innocence of just walking the trail and being in my own little happy bubble and then getting hit by the reality of life.

Turkey tail: unknown, mystery, unsettled

When I woke up this morning, I was still unsettled because of the accident from the previous day. I was also really uncomfortable because there were so many people on the trail. One of the reasons I do these long-distance walks is to escape the busyness of everyday life and relax into the solitude of nature. I felt a bit disappointed with myself for not planning the route better in terms of my starting days.

This is a popular portion of the trail where there are a lot of hill forts and sights, which draw a lot of people out on the weekend. I was also unsettled by all these people because I had gotten accustomed to having such a quiet time on route. "Unsettled" definitely describes this day.

Cannabis: revelry, fun, time off

I can't say that this was a particularly fun day on the trail, but it is a segment of the trail that I really love. I went to see Wayland's Smithy in the morning, I saw hill forts along the way, and I think I was finally sinking back into the happiness and the joy of being alone on the path. It was like the fear and paranoia, and unsettledness had bubbled up and out of my system.

Catnip: opposites, separation, contrast

This was my final day on the Ridgeway. I knew I was nearing the end of the trail; it ended before I reached my accommodation in East Kennet. So "separation" was the perfect theme for the day. It was that post-trail sadness that was caused by the separation of this beautiful liminal space where I had existed on my own for the last seven days. It was a lovely day, but I was also sad to reach the end of the trail.

Stinging nettle: sacrifice, reward, pain

This was the extra day where I walked around Avebury, which is one of my special places to visit. I reconnected with some trees from my book and revisited all my favorite sites in the area. The pain I felt would be the grief and sadness of finishing the trail, and the reward would be all the beautiful memories I would have from the journey and of the revisiting of my favorite places in Avebury.

Knotweed: defenses, resiliency, preparation

The overarching theme was knotweed, which represents "defenses, resiliency, and preparation." When I first pulled these oracle cards, I was really on edge about them because they didn't seem like very fun cards. But in reality, these are cards that really represent the ups-and-downs of an inner journey and transformation: defenses and resiliency.

"Defenses" represents all the fear I had that was bubbling up along the trail, and my resiliency was my determination to carry on. On that was one day where I was so paranoid about that man, there was a point where I actually thought: "Is it safe for me to carry on? Should I quit walking? Should I stop posting pictures about this on Instagram?" I actually thought about pausing my journey. I am glad I didn't because that would have meant that fear was taking over my life.

I feel like all the preparation I have done came from my previous walking and preparing to do it in a way, taking all the breaks I needed and taking care of my feet, I didn't get any blisters this time around, which I am super proud of. I feel like my preparation and my experience really paid off.

I'M SO happy that I decided to re-visit the Ridgeway in 2020. It was the perfect outdoor adventure to split up the two major COVID-19 lockdowns that we had in 2020 in the UK. The trail gave me a much-needed break from the solitude of lockdown life, and I'm convinced that it gave me a solid foundation that boosted my mental health during the isolation of the winter shut-in. Winter felt even darker, wetter, and muddier than ever, and I longed to be out on a big adventure—which wasn't allowed at the time.

Simply revisiting my Ridgeway journey when I was editing this book for publication helped. Wherever you are as you read this, I hope that it gives you a boost, too. May it give you many exciting ideas for joyful adventures in the outdoors! Happy trails to you.

PART III

PLANNING

WHAT TO EXPECT

The previous chapters of this book should have given you an idea of what the Ridgeway experience is like. The following chapters will give you more details of the technical bits you'll need for planning a walk.

On the Ridgeway, you can expect the following:

- On the western half of the trail: wide, open byways with little shade. Views of never-ending farmland and gorgeous fields of grain. Small villages with few services.
- On the eastern half of the trail: shady, narrow footpaths and trails that wind through woodland. Larger towns and villages, and generally more services.
- A wealth of ancient historical sites, from stone circles to long barrows to tumuli, particularly on the western half.
- Excellent signage, though it's always a good idea to bring a guidebook with maps and the relevant OS maps or A to Z Adventure book.

- Not much water along the way. No lake views, no sea views, no rivers to ford. Water taps are few and far between.
- Mostly natural trails, with very little tarmac to walk on—even on the byways.
- Occasional stretches of busy roads, which can be jarring after the extreme solitude of the trail.
- Hours upon hours of glorious nature, giving you the feeling of being enveloped by never-ending fields, with the only sign of civilization being farms or tiny villages off in the distance.
- The Ridgeway is much more remote than the South Downs Way, especially on the western half, which feels beautifully removed from urban life.
- Accommodation ranging from tiny inns, B&Bs, and the occasional youth hostel. Camping is an option all along the route.

If any of this sounds like it's what you're looking for in a long-distance trail, I highly recommend you plan to walk the Ridgeway. It's a relatively easy trail, with so much to offer.

LESSONS LEARNED

Plan, plan, plan in advance to make your walk as enjoyable and pain-free as you possibly can, especially if it's your first long-distance trail. I learned so much from my South Downs Way, Downs Link, and Wey-South Path walks—and I was able to put it all into practice on my Ridgeway adventures.

New things I learned on the Ridgeway

Plan for shorter walking distances each day, so you can spend more time at historical sites and other attractions and even make detours off the trail to visit interesting places. This is particularly important on the western half of the trail.

Carry extra water to keep your head cool when it's hot outside—this is especially important in the summer months.

If you can, space your walking days evenly in terms of distance. It's a bit disappointing to have such a short final day of walking. Thankfully, I was able to remedy this on my second Ridgeway journey.

Don't automatically assume the stages recommended by

your guidebook are right for you without calculating the distance you'll need to walk each day. On my first journey, I did a variation on the medium-paced itinerary from my guidebook, adding an extra day to break up a long 17-mile (27 km) day in the beginning. On my second journey, 17 miles was much more doable, so I had a couple of longer days.

Ask yourself

Are you sure the Ridgeway is right for you? Maybe you'd prefer a different National Trail or national park, or somewhere else entirely. Does the Ridgeway have what you want in terms of local history, scenery, and accommodations?

What are your reasons for walking the Ridgeway? What do you want to get out of it? Is this for fun, to go on a solo retreat, or are you looking to get some exercise outdoors? Or is it something else?

Who do you want to walk with? Are you planning a solo walking holiday, as I did, or would you rather go with a partner or friends?

When do you want to walk the Ridgeway? If your walk falls during British Summer Time, then you'll have long days. But summers can be hot. Perhaps consider late spring after BST starts or early autumn before the time changes again. My favorite months for walking are now April and September.

How are you going to walk the Ridgeway? Are you a daywalker at heart, a weekend walker, or a through walker? Maybe you'd like to split it in half between the western and eastern portions? You don't have to do it all at once.

How do you want to walk it? From west to east, or the other way around?

Plan well

Asking yourself the above questions and getting clear on your answers can help you to plan well. You'll need to plan your trip before you book, before you pack, and before you start out each day. When you're out on a long-distance walk, you can't plan enough—especially if you're walking alone.

Things to consider when booking accommodation: how far off the trail your lodging is and how you want to spend the night (B&B, inn, hostel, camping). If your accommodation is more than a mile off the Ridgeway, you can plan to walk on the trail to the closest point to that village and get transport if you're tired (a good guidebook will give you an idea of whether this is possible).

In general, make sure your lodging is as close as possible to the Ridgeway: in a village that's close to the trail, and within that village, whichever accommodation is the closest to the trail. Avoid extra walking if you're new to long-distance walking —or plan to have a shorter day on the trail. Be sure to count this distance off the trail in your total miles or kilometers for each day: you'll need to get back to the Ridgeway in the morning and then come off the trail in the evening. It all adds up.

Plan your packing list well, and carefully evaluate everything before you put your pack together. Once you're ready, weigh your pack (including two to three quarts/liters of water and any snacks you plan to bring) and then re-evaluate the contents of your pack. I've done enough long-distance walks now to know that I'm completely confident about my packing list. I take only what I need and nothing more. But some people tend to over-pack, which will only make things more challenging for you on your journey.

Also, plan ahead to determine whether you'll want to carry your water in bottles or in a bladder/reservoir. I ended up getting a reservoir for my Downs Link walk. Its easy access through a tube coming just off my shoulder strap meant that I rehydrated early and often because all I needed to do to take a sip of water was to turn my head. However, because the water bladder is located within my pack, I can't see how much I've been drinking, so it's hard to pace myself.

If I'm walking with only a water bladder, I have to rely strictly on thirst to keep hydrated, rather than setting goals to drink a certain amount by a specific time. That's why my preferred method now is to carry both a water reservoir and a one-liter water bottle. I sip on the water hose as I walk, and I take a long drink of water from the bottle when I stop for a rest.

Some people complain about the water bladder making the water taste like plastic, but mine doesn't change the water's taste. Plus, it has a wide opening, which allows me to add a tray of ice cubes, keeping the water cool for hours. I've never had access to ice while on the trail, but if I know it's going to be hot, I'll leave home with ice in my water on the first day.

The night before each day's walk, review your route for the following day and note the conditions: weather, temperature, water taps, facilities, etc. If rain is forecast, be sure your waterproofs are easily accessible. If it's going to be scorching hot and there are no water taps, plan to bring more water than you think you'll need.

Lastly, are you a woman who might start her monthly cycle while on the walk? I did when I was on the South Downs Way, and thankfully I managed to plan my Ridgeway walks at a different time of the month. If you can't imagine dealing with menstruation out in the wild, be sure to plan your walk later in your cycle. You may also notice that you have lower energy levels on the first day or two of your cycle. I now track my cycle, and I know that I'm a bit more tired and lethargic at the very start of each cycle. However, I've also noticed that my sports performance is much better in the first half of my cycle, from

Day 2 up to ovulation. That's important to know if you're planning a long walk.

Plan in advance

In 2016, I planned my trip about two months in advance, but in 2020 I booked three months in advance, making it much easier to find accommodation in all the places I wanted to stay. Weekends are the most challenging time to get accommodation in the summer, and if you can, try to not start your walk on the weekend. Start on a Sunday or Monday instead. That way, you won't start or end your walk on the busiest nights of Friday or Saturday.

I live close enough to the Ridgeway that I was able to get a ride to Avebury in 2016 and start my walk that same day, and then get a ride home from Ivinghoe on my final day. In 2020, I did the same, but the other way around. But you live further away, or you need to use public transport, you might need an extra day's accommodation at the start and end of your journey.

Avebury is equidistant from both Swindon and Pewsey rail stations for arrival at the start of the Ridgeway. Swindon is probably your best bet if you'd like to take a bus to Avebury (just under an hour's journey). Pewsey is just a 20-minute drive away, so while it's not as convenient by bus, you could arrange a taxi from that rail station. Tring is your nearest rail station at the end, with a direct line to London Euston, just a 35-45 minute journey.

Avoid suffering

Because my Ridgeway walk was free of suffering—though I did experience a bit of soreness and blisters the first time around—I'm borrowing this section of the book from my South Downs Way book, which was a much more painful experience.

Suffering is optional, but you need to plan a bit more if you really want to avoid it. Figure out your pain points by asking yourself what might make you miserable when walking, and plan ahead to avoid it. Think about sore muscles, aching feet, blisters, shoulder and back pain, headaches, sunburn, and heat. Most of these issues can be avoided if you plan well in advance. This section is not an exhaustive description of how to avoid each particular malaise and is just intended to be an introduction, so please do your own research online.

General soreness can be avoided by buying a great backpack that fits you well, great shoes/boots (that fit you and which allow extra room for thick walking socks), and by packing light. Of course, this is assuming that you're already in walking shape and that you're accustomed to heading up and down hills regularly. If not, you'll want to get in shape before you go. This takes time. If you don't have enough time to really get in shape and you still want to risk it, pack some ibuprofen and a small tube of arnica cream to deal with the consequences.

Blisters are generally caused by friction and can be avoided by having good fitting shoes/boots (mine are a full size larger than my regular shoes) and the appropriate socks, by taking your socks off to air them and your feet out at breaks, and by breaking your shoes in for at least 100 miles before your main walk. Be sure to read up online on all the ways to avoid blisters, as they can really make your walk miserable. If you do end up with blisters, be sure you've got alcohol to clean them off, a sewing kit with a needle you can drain the blisters with (I know you're not supposed to do this, but I do), and a collection of Compeed in different sizes to cover your blisters. Compeed is a lifesaver.

Shoulder and back pain can be avoided with a lightweight pack that fits you well. I got lucky with my backpack (an Osprey Kyte 36), as it fits me so well it feels like it's part of my body. Ideally, you want to go into a shop and try on different packs, but I got both of my packs online (I have a smaller, 26-liter pack for day walks), and they're perfect.

Headaches can be avoided by wearing a good sun hat (preferably one with a chin strap for wind) and staying adequately hydrated. I wore my sun hat for about 95% of the time I was on the trail. The only time I put it in my pack was during rain when I had my waterproof jacket and hood on, and that one morning when it was gray and misty. I'm particularly sensitive to the sun on my head, so I always keep covered when I'm out on a walk. Still, be sure to take your preferred headache remedy just in case.

Sunburn is an easy one: bring sunscreen at an appropriate strength for your skin. I had a small tube of SPF 50, and I still have some left. If you're wearing long pants, you'll just need to worry about your hands, arms, face, ears, and neck. Remember that if you're using walking poles, your hands and lower arms will be more exposed to the sun than usual. I applied sunscreen at least twice daily to the backs of my hands, in addition to all the usual areas, and more frequently on the super hot days when I was sweating off all the sunscreen.

Train in advance

If you've never done a long-distance walk before, you might want to do a trial walk of perhaps 2-3 days. If you're based in southeast England, the Downs Link trail is a good option for this: it connects the North Downs Way with the South Downs Way and is easily done over three days. My book, Walking the Downs Link: Planning Guide & Reflections on Walking from St. Martha's Hill to Shoreham-by-Sea, details my own walk.

The Wey-South Path is another excellent option for a 2-3 day walk. It's flat and shady and very easy going. I enjoyed it even more than I did the Downs Link. And I have a book about this trail, too: Walking the Wey-South Path: Planning Guide & Reflections on Walking from Guildford to Amberley.

You can also do a series of 2-3 day walks back to back, based from your home. If you're based in Britain, Catherine Redfern has put together a series of weekend walks called Walk Your Weekend. You can purchase these detailed weekend guides from her website.

The critical detail for these walks is to load up your pack with the kind of weight you'll be bringing on a long-distance journey to help you get used to walking with a heavier pack. I also now add extra weight to my pack when I'm doing a day walk. That little bit extra helps with the training.

Water is a delicate balance

Water is heavy, and it's a delicate balance between carrying too much (and thus hauling around too much weight) and not enough (and risking your life to dehydration, heat exhaustion, and heat stroke). Plan each day carefully, studying your guidebook or map the night before to see if there are any water taps or restaurants along the way to fill up your water supply. This will mean you won't have to depart in the morning with your full water supply.

However, there are many stretches of the Ridgeway that have no water taps or restaurants at all. If you plan your itinerary as I did, you'll have to leave your B&B in the morning with all your water, which could be three to four quarts/liters, depending on the weather. Take hydration seriously, and plan ahead.

Always bring more water than you think you'll need. I can't say this enough. It adds extra weight, but you don't want to risk your life to heatstroke or dehydration.

PACKING LIST

As I did with my previous walking books, I've split my list into items I used daily, items I used some days, and items I never used. I'm also providing commentary on what I plan to do differently on my next long-distance walk. Your packing list will be different depending on your needs, but many of the items will be similar.

Items I used every day

Arnica cream: I used Arnica cream on my South Downs Way walk, and it's been my wonder cream ever since. I slather it on all my aching bits (legs and feet) at the end of the day, before going to bed.

Backpack: Mine is an Osprey Kyte 36, and it is perfect in so many ways. It's just the right size, and it fits me perfectly. I've used it on all of my long-distance walks, and it's been wonderful each time. If you decide on an Osprey, you can browse their website and select a pack based on the level of importance of features such as: women's specific fit (if relevant to you), lightweight, torso adjustability, integrated rain cover, trampoline-mesh style back system to keep you cool, and the maximum number of entry points, pockets, and organization, among other things. I like the integrated rain cover on my Kyte, and it's got lots of entry points to store things, which is convenient.

Bags: I brought a small bag to keep the following things in: my extra set of clothes and all my bathroom stuff: toothbrush, Arnica cream, etc. I have a simple string bag that I use when I go out in the evenings: I put my iPhone, iPad, reading glasses, and wallet in there to go out for dinner.

Birkenstocks: These are the perfect evening shoes, much more comfortable than flip flops, which might rub your feet if you've got a long walk to the pub for dinner. Mine are the Gizeh style, with the toe post. One thing about Birks, they're both comfortable and super light. And the fact that they're open sandals means that your feet can air out. Also, they have excellent arch support for tired feet.

Boots/Shoes: Mine are lightweight Salomon X ULTRA 2 GTX® W shoes, which combine trail running technology with a Gore-Tex hiking shoe. Note that this is a very old model, and an updated version is available. These shoes are much cooler than my Meindl boots that I wore on the South Downs Way, and they are my preferred walking shoe for spring, summer, and fall walking. The only time I wear my hiking boots now is in the winter, or when I know it will be muddy.

Clothes: I brought two sets of walking clothes. In the daytime, I wore my standard walking pants, which are Craghoppers Women's NosiLife trousers. They are my standard walking pants for spring, summer, and fall walking. In the winter, I wear Craghoppers Women's Kiwi Pro Stretch Lined trousers, which are fleece lined.

For tops, I brought two short sleeve sports layers that were thin, cool, and easy to dry, and often dried overnight in my room, even without a heated towel rack. I brought two low-impact sports bras (not the kind that are designed for lots of running or bouncing), two pairs of underwear (I don't recommend cotton as they don't wick the sweat from your body), and four pairs of socks. I alternated between two pairs of socks every day, then washed them both at night and used two fresh pairs the following day.

Clothes drying system: I invented this myself, so there might be something better out there. However, everyone who has seen it on my walks seems to think it's a sound system for drying clothes while walking. It consists of three binder clips attached to a key ring, which then hooks onto the backpack with a carabiner. I use one clip for each sock and the third for my sports bra. Underwear usually dries overnight in my room.

Glasses: I brought reading glasses for reading books on my iPad in the evenings, but I did not bring sunglasses, as I don't usually use them. If I didn't use a specific prescription with different strength in each eye, I would buy the kind of reading glasses that fold up into a tiny box, as they'd take up less space and weight that way.

Guidebook & Maps: I recommend a guidebook and maps in the Resources section.

Lip balm: Normally, I never use lip balm because I drink enough water to keep my skin hydrated. But if it's hot and sunny when you're walking the Ridgeway, you'll want to bring some. I used mine every single day, multiple times a day. Be sure it has sun protection in it.

Pills: I used a small Ziploc baggie to bring my medication, vitamins, and supplements. I just brought enough for the time I'd be walking, and I brought only the things that were absolutely necessary, like magnesium, which really helps me with muscle recovery after exercise.

Poles: I use Pacerpoles, designed by physiotherapist Heather Rhodes, who is based up in Windermere (Cumbria, in northern England). These are the best poles I've seen. Pacerpoles help give you better posture when walking, promote better breathing, better stability (they've saved me from tripping and falling many times). These poles have the best handgrip of any poles I've seen. They're designed for a relaxed hand position with minimal grip, and they make getting up hills much more comfortable. I highly recommend them.

Sun hat or Buff: I've got a good hat from Columbia with a wide brim and a chin strap for the wind. Not super attractive, but I'm sensitive to the sun on my head, and even if you think you aren't, you'll want to bring one. Sun safety is essential. These days, I often wear a Buff on my head, which mostly protects me from the sun.

Tech: I brought my iPad mini in its case, which includes a small keyboard, and its charger. I had to bring a separate USB cable to charge the keyboard. I also brought my iPhone with its charger and USB cable. The iPad was easy to slide down the side of my backpack, and I stored all the cords and chargers in a little bag. I used the iPad to write this book and to read, as I had loaded a couple of new books onto it before I left. For future walks, I'll definitely bring it, as long as I'm staying in B&Bs and places where I can charge. I also brought headphones in case I wanted to listen to music in the evenings.

Tissues: My hay fever wasn't bothering me as much on the Ridgeway as it did on the South Downs Way, but these are good to have.

Toiletries: I kept these to a minimum: sunscreen in a small tube, travel-sized toothpaste, toothbrush, hand sanitizer for cleaning off and draining blisters. This is all stuff I'd bring again. Most hotels had liquid or bar soap and shampoo, but if you're staying at hostels, you'll need your own.

Wallet: Just before I was getting ready to leave, I transferred the essentials to a much smaller wallet: a bit of cash and three cards, including my National Trust membership card, essential for Avebury.

Water: I brought the Osprey Hydraulics™ LT 2.5L Reservoir, which I love. I've heard the water doesn't always taste that great in a bladder, but that's not a problem with this brand. It makes it easy to carry water on your back, so you've got easy access to it via a tube that comes over your shoulder and clips to your backpack strap.

Items I used some days

Compeed: I will always bring Compeed blister plasters on a walk like this. It's not cheap, but it's worth every penny. Get more of this stuff than you think you'll need.

Fleece: Instead of bringing the long-sleeved base layer that I

brought on the South Downs Way, I brought a very lightweight
fleece. If you purchase a fleece that has a full zip, it's more
versatile, and you can manage your temperature better.

Pen: I brought a ballpoint pen and mostly used it to make notes
for this book.

Snacks: After I brought too many snacks on the South Downs
Way, I brought just one small bag of nuts on this walk. I didn't
need more than that.

Travel sewing kit: This was essential in my blister care: I used
the pins in the sewing kit to drain blisters (which I know you're
not supposed to do, but everyone seems to do it anyway—
including myself). The one I have is tiny and lightweight. I
bought it more for blisters than for sewing.

Waterproofs: I have a North Face waterproof jacket and
Berghaus waterproof pants. I only wore them on the first day.
Still, I never go walking in England without waterproofs, so I'll
definitely bring them on future walks.

Items I never used

Asthma inhaler: Asthma is an on and off problem for me, and
it's generally brought on by allergies such as hay fever, so I
always make sure to have an inhaler with me if I'm going on a
walk.

Compass: Didn't use it once. It's one of those essential things
you must have, though. I have definitely used it on my day
walks. While the iPhone does have a compass app, it often

doesn't work well in remote areas, which is when you need it most. I'll definitely bring this again.

Emergency shelter: I've never actually had to use this, but I always have it with me now. It's a small, two-person shelter, big enough to fit me and my backpack inside.

First aid kit: I brought a very compact one I found online and never used it, but this is another one of those things that you've really got to have around, just in case.

Flashlight: I never used this. I walked during BST, so there was really no risk of being out on the trail after dark, but this is another of those just in case things that you need to have. A headlamp is most convenient for outdoor adventures.

House keys: This seemed like unnecessary weight because Agustín walked me to and from the rail station when I left and arrived, but I wanted to be sure I could get back in the house in case his plans changed for my return, and he couldn't be there.

Knife: I never used this, but this is another of those just in case things that you need to have.

Whistle: I never used this, but this is yet another of those just in case things that you need to have. Do you know the signal for distress? It's six good long blasts. Stop for one minute. Repeat. Continue in this manner until someone reaches you, and don't stop just because you've heard a reply – your rescuers may be using your whistle blasts as a way to figure out exactly where you are.

WHEN TO WALK

The weather in southeast England is relatively mild compared to other parts of the country. If you're experienced in walking in cold weather, you might be open to exploring the Ridgeway at any time of the year. However, you'll probably find it most enjoyable between April and September. Summer in England is totally unpredictable, and the hot and sunny weather that I experienced during my walk would have been impossible to plan for (or to avoid).

If you want to avoid the possibility of such great heat (and thus the need to carry large quantities of water), you may prefer to book your walk in April or September, when it's less likely to be so warm. England is not, of course, known for its sunny climate, so whether you choose to walk during summer or not, you'll want to carry a waterproof jacket and pants with you for protection from the rain. Walking for hours on end in wet clothing makes for a miserable experience, and it's worth the extra weight to carry the waterproofs. Statistically speaking, July and August should be the driest months. They are also the warmest months.

Remember that the western half of the Ridgeway is relatively open and exposed to the elements (meaning: sun and wind). In contrast, the eastern half is more woodsy and protected.

WHERE TO STAY

One thing I learned when I walked the South Downs Way was to stay as close as possible to the trail, and to stay in a place as central as possible within the village (rather than on the outskirts) to avoid extra walking between the trail and the B&B and to and from dinner in the evenings. When I've walked twelve to fifteen miles during the day, I really don't want an extra walk added on at the end. Luckily, I managed to put this into practice when planning my Ridgeway walk, and it made for a much more comfortable experience.

Also, remember that there are many different ways to split up the Ridgeway into stages. You can walk it in five, seven, or nine days—or however you choose. And even if you choose an eight-day walk as I did in 2016 and a seven-day walk in 2020 (plus one extra day around Avebury), you may decide to split the stages up differently. Consult a guidebook and at least a couple of websites for different options on how to split up your walk.

Unlike my experience on the South Downs Way, it seemed that many of the places that I stayed on the Ridgeway accepted card payments. This may be because I stayed at more inns and pubs and at fewer B&Bs, or it may just be particular of this area. Note that some places will require a bank deposit or a credit card to reserve the room. If you're confident that you won't be changing dates or canceling your trip, I highly recommend paying the full amount rather than just the deposit. This will reduce the amount of cash you need to carry with you to pay for your room balance and food.

You'll see that you can also book a room online at many of these places, which is often the deciding factor in planning walking accommodation for me. It can be challenging to plan a walk when you've got to phone a B&B, leave a message, and wait for the owner to get back to you. Online booking makes the planning process much more manageable. If I know that a place offers this, I'll often choose it over other, possibly nicer, accommodation that requires you to book via phone call.

Here's my list of suggested accommodations, from west to east.

East Kennett

When I first planned to spend an extra day in Avebury and the surrounding area before starting my Ridgeway walk, I looked at staying in Avebury village, which I now know wouldn't have been at all convenient. East Kennet was the perfect place to stay, as it lay right on the path coming down from the West Kennet Long Barrow and toward the Sanctuary and the start of the Ridgeway at Overton Hill. If you use the Trailblazer guide, as I did, you'll find The Old Forge right on the map of the "walk around Avebury." Excellent location.

I absolutely loved my stay at The Old Forge. It was the prettiest room that I stayed in on my Ridgeway walk, which is both good and bad: while I always enjoy a pretty, comfortable place to stay, an extra nice room — especially when it's in somebody's home — always makes me feel uncomfortable when I arrive muddy and dirty from the trail. I paid £75 for my room, which included breakfast.

If you decide to start your Ridgeway walk on a Monday, as I did, and stay at The Old Forge on a Sunday night, remember that you'll have to hop in a taxi and travel to Marlborough for dinner. Or you could plan to pick up something for dinner at the shop in Avebury so you can eat in your room, without leaving the B&B. There's a fridge in your room, where you can store food.

You can book your room online via their website.

Ogbourne St. George

The Inn with the Well isn't more than 15 minutes off the trail. I've now stayed here three times, and it's perfect for walkers. With its boot tray just inside the door to the room, the Inn with the Well was clearly used to hosting walkers, which is always good. Still, its most important feature was the heated towel rack, with three heated bars to dry clothes on overnight. Dinner and breakfast were also excellent, as was the large packed lunch. I paid £70 for my room, which included breakfast. If you book directly through them, ask about a 10% discount—and you may end up with a free pint, too.

You can book your room online via their website.

Ashbury

When planning my 2016 Ridgeway walk, I had initially wanted to stay in Bishopstone, the turnoff for which is just ahead of Ashbury's turn off on the trail. However, both The Royal Oak and Prebendal Farm, the only two places to stay mentioned in my guidebook, were closed, and I couldn't find anything else online, so I opted for Ashbury instead. The Rose & Crown, where I stayed, is just a half-mile (.8 km) off the trail, down one of two pretty footpaths.

The Rose & Crown was renovated by its new owners in 2016. My room was incredibly spacious and comfortable, with much more space than I needed. My guidebook states that it's a popular place for Ridgeway walkers to stay, and I definitely felt comfortable there—not at all out of place. However, I appeared to be the only walker staying at the time. I paid £65 for my room, which included breakfast.

Note that if you arrive while the pub is closed in the afternoon, you'll have to walk around to the back door and phone their off-hours number to get someone to open up for you. The good news is that you can wait in the shade of their garden for them to let you in. Dinner and breakfast were excellent, as was the packed lunch. Also, be aware that if you stay there on a Sunday, you'll have to plan in advance for dinner, as they don't serve an evening meal on that day—and there's nowhere else in the village to get food on Sundays.

You can book your room online via their website.

Court Hill

In 2016, I initially planned to book my stay in Letcombe Regis, located 1.5 miles (2.4 km) from the Ridgeway. However, I opted for the Court Hill Centre instead, for two reasons: it's much closer to the trail, and I wanted to see if I could handle staying at a youth hostel again. While Court Hill Centre is very comfortable, especially when it's virtually empty, hosteling is definitely not for me. I was so stressed out at the thought of having to share a room with other people after hours of peace and quiet on the trail that I won't be taking this risk again.

However, if you don't mind sharing a room, or if you plan on camping, the Court Hill Centre is perfect. The tea room is nice for a cup of tea at the end of a long day's walk, the courtyard is perfect to relax outdoors in the afternoon, and the meals are very inexpensive and good. The staff are very, very friendly.

I paid £41 total, which included my room, dinner, breakfast, *and* a packed lunch.

You'll have to phone to book a room. See their website for more details. They appear to have an online booking system, but their calendar always appears fully booked, even when that's not the case.

Wantage

If you can't get a room at Court Hill, or if you don't feel like staying at a youth hostel, you can stay in the nearby village of Wantage (about 1 3/4 miles or 2.8 km from The Ridgeway), which is what I did in 2020. I really didn't love The Bear Hotel, so you might want to check out other options in Wantage before booking. Alfred's Lodge and The Bear Inn are centrally located, and you might find an Airbnb that works for you. Wantage is a great place to stop if you need to re-fuel or purchase anything, as it's quite a large town.

Goring

Melrose Cottage is a very comfortable and very affordable B&B with a lovely owner. If you are staying here, don't walk through town to reach the B&B via the High Street. Instead, keep going along the Ridgeway, and turn off it down Mill Road, then turn right on Wallingford Road, then left on Milldown Road, where Melrose Cottage is located. It's a much quicker method of access than what I did. Check it out on Google Maps before you go, so you understand how to find the B&B.

My room was comfortable, with a ceiling fan to keep cool, a small fridge, and a bathroom just next door. Breakfast was delicious. I paid £40 for my room, which included breakfast. You'll have to phone to book a room: 01491 873040.

In 2020 I stayed at an Airbnb, which was perfectly situated just minutes from the Ridgeway. It was only ten minutes or so into the main part of the village for dinner.

Watlington

If you are staying in Watlington, be sure to take the right road into town. Do not take the busy B480 road, which I did in 2016, but rather the much quieter Hill Road, which is a little bit farther down the Ridgeway (if you're walking from west to east). Both are clearly marked on the Trailblazer guide map; make yourself familiar with the landmarks, and you'll have a much more pleasant walk into Watlington than I did. If you're walking from east to west, you'll come across Hill Road first, so it's harder to miss.

Having said that, there aren't many options for accommodation here, and I highly recommend the Fat Fox Inn, where I stayed. Small, comfortable room. Nice bathroom, and most importantly: a heated towel rack to dry my clothes. I paid £75 for my room, which included breakfast.

Excellent dinner and breakfast, though they only provide a simple sandwich, and not a full packed lunch—though this might have changed now that the place is (thankfully) under new management. There are also plenty of shops in the village to buy your lunch.

You can book your room online via their website.

Princes Risborough

There aren't many options here, and the place where I stayed in 2016 is now closed (though you didn't miss much).

The Ridgeway Lodge B&B (not to be confused with the

retirement home of the same name) is located right on the Ridgeway trail, which makes for easy access, but they don't offer dinner, so either plan ahead to eat in your room, or walk 1.5 miles (2.4 km) to the Princes Risborough High Street to get food at the M&S or at a local restaurant. You can check availability and send a booking enquiry via their website: https://www.bedbreakfast-ridgewaylodge.co.uk/.

The other option is Bakehouse Farm House, where I've never stayed. It can be reserved through Booking.com.

There may be one Airbnb property available; be sure to check that website if you can't find anything else.

Wendover

Rather than staying in Tring, you might want to stay in Wendover, which has a few accommodation options. This little village has several shops and restaurants, making it an excellent place to stay the night. Plus, The Ridgeway goes straight through it.

I really enjoyed the Red Lion Hotel when I stayed there in 2020. My room was simple and comfortable, and dinner was quite good. If you book directly with them, you'll get a 10% discount.

Tring

Located just a half-mile (less than 1 km) from the Ridgeway, Pendley Manor used to be an ideal stop for your last night on the trail—but then it was renovated, and prices skyrocketed. It's more of a wedding venue than a walker's rest stop, but it's conveniently located. The room rate apparently includes access to their indoor heated pool, which might be nice if you've got room in your pack for a swimsuit. Spa treatments are also available, though advance booking is recommended.

My room in 2016—before renovation—was large, as was the bathroom. Though the furnishings were outdated, it was quiet and comfortable, even though the hotel was full of wedding parties. There was a pedestal fan in the room, which kept it cool.

Dinner and breakfast were excellent. You'll probably want to have your dinner in the Shakespeare Bar as I did, rather than in their main dining room unless you've got room in your pack for "smart casual" clothes. Their bar menu has a wide variety of options, and the food is delicious.

You can book online via their website.

There are a couple of other options in the main village, and you might want to check Airbnb to see if there's anything available. However, Tring is so close to Ivinghoe Beacon that I wouldn't recommend staying there as it makes for a very short first or last day on the Ridgeway.

BUDGET

In 2016, I initially budgeted about £700 for the nine days. This broke down into eight nights of accommodation at £65 each night, and eight days of food at £25 per day. Note that I got a ride to and from the trail, so that wasn't a part of my budget.

In total, I spent £512 on accommodation and about £20-25 each day on food: lunch was consistently £6, and dinner came in just under £20 each evening. Breakfast was always included with my accommodation, though I had to supplement the poor breakfast that was offered in Princes Risborough with a trip to M&S.

The total cost for my journey came in just under my original estimate, at roughly £674. This does not include any gear, as I had all of it already. I'd say this is a mid-range budget, and you could spend more or less depending on where you stay and where and what you choose to eat and drink. Inns will be less expensive than B&Bs, and hostels and camping will cost even less. Most guidebooks will show you accommodation options in all price ranges.

Keep in mind that there are no banks in the villages you'll

be staying in along the western portion of the Ridgeway. Interestingly, more places accepted credit/debit cards along the Ridgeway than along the South Downs Way, despite the trail's remoteness. However, always check in advance when you're booking to make sure, and carry extra cash just in case.

Unlike the South Downs Way, where accommodation prices really spiked between 2015 and 2019, my accommodation along The Ridgeway in 2020 came in at £526, which isn't much over my 2016 budget. However, I did spend one less night on the trail. Dinner was about £20-25, and I didn't get lunch every day like I had on my first journey.

SAFETY

Everyone I speak with about my long-distance walks seems impressed that I do so much walking on my own. It's my preferred way to walk: I relish the quiet meditative aspect that comes with solo walking in nature. It helps me to relax and to reconnect with myself. It's a deeply transformational experience.

If you choose to walk alone, you need to be aware that you must be totally self-reliant: be vigilant about the weather, the temperature, and your water supply, especially when walking in the warmer months of the year. You must be sure that you set out each morning with more than enough water to drink and food to keep you going until you arrive at your evening destination. I cannot stress this enough, having walked during a sweltering sunny week in August.

Obviously, follow your own common sense, and stay aware of your surroundings. And remember: only you are responsible for your own personal safety. Make your own decisions, and make them wisely.

Before embarking on a long-distance walk like this, you should be sure that you're physically fit to safely complete the

walk and that you have sought medical advice if you have not
exercised for some time or if you are suffering from any
medical condition.

However...if you're reasonably fit and healthy and you're
aware of the risks of walking outdoors, you should be fine. If
you're still not convinced that it's safe to walk on your own,
Catherine Redfern of London Hiker has a blog post detailing
Why you CAN (and should) go hiking on your own. Check
it out.

Main risks

When walking a long-distance trail, the main risks include
animals, dehydration, weather, heat and cold injuries, getting
lost, and injury. In England, the most dangerous animal is
probably the cow, which kills 5-6 people on average each year. I
suspect that most of these are dog walkers, who can stress out
cows when they're with their calves. If you're afraid of cows, do
some research about what to do when you come across them
on a trail.

Dehydration is easy to avoid: carry enough water, and drink
it. Remember that hydration is also about electrolytes, so you
may want to carry electrolyte powder with you and add it to
your water. I often carry a small container of pink salt with me
in my backpack—sodium is one type of electrolyte.

Always check the weather before you embark on your journey, each night before going to bed, and each morning when
you get up. Know what to expect before it hits you: whether it's
heat and sunshine or pounding rain. I know this sounds ridiculous, but do not underestimate how hot it can be in England
when you're walking alone out in the sun: carry more than
enough water, and cover your head.

Being aware of the weather can also help you to prevent
heat and cold injuries. Always carry a sun hat or Buff for your

head, and be sure you have extra layers for cooler weather. Bring a hat, scarf or neck warmer, and gloves if you're walking in the colder months. If the weather takes a turn for the worse, consider getting off the trail rather than pushing on.

A friend once told me the story of a woman who set out from Avebury to walk the Ridgeway right as a big storm called the Beast from the East came through. She insisted on starting the trail, even though it was snowing. Soon enough, she couldn't even see the trail, and she had to get off the Ridgeway and abandon her journey.

Getting lost is an issue in the outdoors, but it's pretty hard to get lost on the Ridgeway. Just pay attention to the signs. It's still a good idea to carry a map and a compass, just in case.

You also need to be aware that walking and hiking outdoors exposes you to the risks of cardiovascular exercise, injuries from falls, falling branches, and other risks that can occur depending on weather conditions such as wind, rain, ice, heat, or any other severe weather. Trails may be muddy and slippery, and this increases the risk. It's a good idea to train in outdoor first aid, so you know what to do if you get injured.

The 10 essentials

These are items that you should carry with you at all times. I've already mentioned some of these above, but let's go through them systematically.

Navigation: carry a map and a compass, and know how to use them. Use technology like a GPS device or OS Maps app as a backup.

First aid: always bring a first aid kit with you, with extra things like blister plasters or Compeed.

Fire: be sure to have a means of making fire, like matches (keep them dry), a lighter, or a fire steel.

Shelter: I always carry an emergency shelter with me when I go out for a day hike or a long-distance walk. If you search for "emergency bivvy" online, you can find them in all sizes. A two-person shelter will fit you and your backpack, and it can keep you warm if the weather turns bad and you can't evacuate for some reason.

Light: Carry a headlamp or hand-held flashlight. Do not rely on your phone for this. Your phone's light should be a backup.

Knife: you probably won't need it, but it's good to have. Note that the UK knife laws are pretty strict: you'll need a folding blade, which can't be longer than three inches.

Extra food: be sure to have calorie-dense snacks like nuts or protein bars just in case. Remember that if you get into a tricky situation with the weather, eating a snack can keep you warm.

Extra water: by now, you'll know how paranoid I am about water. Be sure you have enough. You won't need a water purifier for the water taps on the Ridgeway, and the only natural source of water is the River Thames, where it passes through Goring and Streatley.

Extra clothes: as mentioned earlier, bring sun protection and cold protection—gloves, scarf or neck warmer, hat, Buff, etc.

Sun protection: be sure to have a hat or Buff for your head, sunscreen for your skin, and SPF lip balm for your lips.

Two-legged predators

When people wonder about the safety of a solo woman walking a long-distance trail, it's two-legged "predators" that they're usually thinking about. I do a lot of solo walking in England, and I almost always feel safe. When I don't, it's usually irrational fears and not a legitimately dangerous situation. Although I got a bit paranoid on my 2020 adventure, there was no time on the Ridgeway when I felt genuinely unsafe or in danger—even during the very long stretches where I was utterly alone, with no other walkers or cyclists crossing my path.

If this is a fear that's preventing you from embarking on your first long-distance trail, there are a few things that you might want to keep in mind. You're more at risk to danger in towns than on the trails—that's where you'll come across more people. Odds are, a predator won't hike miles into the middle of nowhere on the off chance that a solo woman hiker will come by.

Be aware of your surroundings. Don't listen to music, podcasts, or audiobooks in both ears. Either use bone-conducting headphones or use an earbud in just one ear.

If someone approaches you and engages in unwanted conversation, make it clear that you want to walk alone and that you're meeting a friend or partner just up ahead. Don't admit that you're actually alone on the trail. If the person asks you where you're staying or how far you're walking that day, be vague or lie outright. Don't share your plans.

Don't be over-polite, either. Make it clear that you want to be on your own and don't want to talk. Say that you're mulling over a business or work project and that you need to think. Or make up some other excuse.

Listen to your gut. If something doesn't feel right, pay attention to that. Don't let your head override your intuition.

Skills to learn

You might want to learn some outdoor skills to help you feel even more confident on your journey. Look into mountain skills courses, walking leadership courses, and winter skills courses if you'll be walking in the winter.

If you're going to spend much time outdoors, I recommend you take an outdoor first aid course. This is a 16-hour, two-day course that will teach you basic first aid plus outdoor applications.

For navigation, try the National Navigation Award Scheme if you're in the UK. There are three levels of courses: bronze, silver, and gold. You can take a virtual map reading course to get started if you're absolutely new to navigation. Once you learn the necessary skills, you might want to challenge yourself with a night navigation or relocation course.

If you've never camped before and you want to learn wild camping (not technically permitted along the Ridgeway, though it may be tolerated by some landowners), sign up for a course. That's how I first got into camping. I went on a wild camping course in south Wales and got to try out all the gear before buying my own.

Finally, if you're concerned about two-legged predators, take a women's self-defense class like Model Mugging or sign up for a martial art. That will help give you confidence not just on the trail—but in everyday life.

THE COUNTRYSIDE CODE OF 2014

Respect. Protect. Enjoy.

In 2004, the UK Countryside Code replaced the Country Code, which dates back to the 1930s. This document details responsibilities for visitors to the countryside and for those who manage the land. The section that concerns walkers is divided into three main areas: respect other people, protect the natural environment, and enjoy the outdoors. Much of it is common sense for anyone who has grown up in rural areas, but for those who haven't, it's worth reading through, which is why I'm including it in this book. The entire document can be found online, including the section that concerns landowners in rural areas. Reprinted below with permission via the Open Government Licence is the most recent version at time of this publication, dating back to 23 October 2014.

Respect other people

Please respect the local community and other people using the outdoors. Remember your actions can affect people's lives and livelihoods.

Consider the local community and other people enjoying the outdoors

Respect the needs of local people and visitors alike – for example, don't block gateways, driveways or other paths with your vehicle.

When riding a bike or driving a vehicle, slow down or stop for horses, walkers and farm animals and give them plenty of room. By law, cyclists must give way to walkers and horse-riders on bridleways.

Co-operate with people at work in the countryside. For example, keep out of the way when farm animals are being gathered or moved and follow directions from the farmer.

Busy traffic on small country roads can be unpleasant and dangerous to local people, visitors and wildlife - so slow down and where possible, leave your vehicle at home, consider sharing lifts and use alternatives such as public transport or cycling. For public transport information, phone Traveline on 0871 200 22 33 or visit www.traveline.org.uk.

Leave gates and property as you find them and follow paths unless wider access is available

A farmer will normally close gates to keep farm animals in, but may sometimes leave them open so the animals can reach food and water. Leave gates as you find them or follow instructions on signs. When in a group, make sure the last person knows how to leave the gates.

Follow paths unless wider access is available, such as on open country or registered common land (known as 'open access land').

If you think a sign is illegal or misleading such as a 'Private -

No Entry' sign on a public path, contact the local authority.

Leave machinery and farm animals alone – don't interfere with animals even if you think they're in distress. Try to alert the farmer instead.

Use gates, stiles or gaps in field boundaries if you can – climbing over walls, hedges and fences can damage them and increase the risk of farm animals escaping.

Our heritage matters to all of us – be careful not to disturb ruins and historic sites.

Protect the natural environment

We all have a responsibility to protect the countryside now and for future generations, so make sure you don't harm animals, birds, plants or trees and try to leave no trace of your visit. When out with your dog make sure it is not a danger or nuisance to farm animals, horses, wildlife or other people.

Leave no trace of your visit and take your litter home

Protecting the natural environment means taking special care not to damage, destroy or remove features such as rocks, plants and trees. They provide homes and food for wildlife, and add to everybody's enjoyment of the countryside.

Litter and leftover food doesn't just spoil the beauty of the countryside, it can be dangerous to wildlife and farm animals – so take your litter home with you. Dropping litter and dumping rubbish are criminal offences.

Fires can be as devastating to wildlife and habitats as they are to people and property – so be careful with naked flames and cigarettes at any time of the year. Sometimes, controlled fires are used to manage vegetation, particularly on heaths and moors between 1 October and 15 April, but if a fire appears to be unattended then report it by calling 999.

Keep dogs under effective control

When you take your dog into the outdoors, always ensure it does not disturb wildlife, farm animals, horses or other people by keeping it under effective control. This means that you:

- keep your dog on a lead, or
- keep it in sight at all times, be aware of what it's doing and be confident it will return to you promptly on command
- ensure it does not stray off the path or area where you have a right of access
- Special dog rules may apply in particular situations, so always look out for local signs – for example:
- dogs may be banned from certain areas that people use, or there may be restrictions, byelaws or control orders limiting where they can go
- the access rights that normally apply to open country and registered common land (known as 'open access' land) require dogs to be kept on a short lead between 1 March and 31 July, to help protect ground nesting birds, and all year round near farm animals
- at the coast, there may also be some local restrictions to require dogs to be kept on a short lead during the bird breeding season, and to prevent disturbance to flocks of resting and feeding birds during other times of year
- it's always good practice (and a legal requirement on 'open access' land) to keep your dog on a lead around farm animals and horses, for your own safety and for the welfare of the animals. A farmer may shoot a dog which is attacking or chasing farm

animals without being liable to compensate the dog's owner

- however, if cattle or horses chase you and your dog, it is safer to let your dog off the lead – don't risk getting hurt by trying to protect it. Your dog will be much safer if you let it run away from a farm animal in these circumstances and so will you
- everyone knows how unpleasant dog mess is and it can cause infections, so always clean up after your dog and get rid of the mess responsibly –' bag it and bin it'. Make sure your dog is wormed regularly to protect it, other animals and people

Enjoy the outdoors

Even when going out locally, it's best to get the latest information about where and when you can go. For example, your rights to go onto some areas of open access land and coastal land may be restricted in particular places at particular times. Find out as much as you can about where you are going, plan ahead and follow advice and local signs.

Plan ahead and be prepared

You'll get more from your visit if you refer to up-to-date maps or guidebooks and websites before you go. Visit Natural England on GOV.UK or contact local information centres or libraries for a list of outdoor recreation groups offering advice on specialist activities.

You're responsible for your own safety and for others in your care – especially children - so be prepared for natural hazards, changes in weather and other events. Wild animals, farm animals and horses can behave unpredictably if you get too close, especially if they're with their young - so give them plenty of space.

Check weather forecasts before you leave. Conditions can change rapidly especially on mountains and along the coast, so don't be afraid to turn back. When visiting the coast check for tide times at easytide.ukho.gov.uk, don't risk getting cut off by rising tides and take care on slippery rocks and sea-weed.

Part of the appeal of the countryside is that you can get away from it all. You may not see anyone for hours, and there are many places without clear mobile phone signals, so let someone else know where you're going and when you expect to return.

Follow advice and local signs

England has about 190,000 km (118,000 miles) of public rights of way, providing many opportunities to enjoy the natural environment. Get to know the signs and symbols used in the countryside to show paths and open countryside. See the Countryside Code leaflet for more detail.

RESOURCES

Guidebooks & Maps

The Ridgeway: Avebury to Ivinghoe Beacon: A Practical Guide with 53 Maps, Places to Stay, Places to Eat by Nick Hill and Henry Stedman

This is an excellent guidebook for walking from Avebury in the west to Ivinghoe Beacon in the east. There are 53 large-scale maps in the book, including guides to all the villages along the Ridgeway. Most of the maps are handwritten and include a wealth of practical information, such as where water taps are located along the way. This information is invaluable when planning each stage.

Before departing on my journey, I took a handful of high-lighters and colored in different bits on each map: I highlighted the trail in yellow, water taps in blue, warnings in pink (things like "don't miss this turn"), natural points of interest in green, and other details in orange.

This guidebook also includes lists of itineraries of different lengths, depending on whether you want to stay at B&Bs or whether you'll be camping and staying in hostels. Its third edition is from 2012, and it's still pretty accurate. I used the Trailblazer guide on my South Downs Way walk, and I was happy to see that they made a guide for the Ridgeway. I highly recommend this guidebook series.

The Ridgeway A to Z Adventure Series (Adventure Atlas)

This slender map book contains the full Ordnance Survey maps in a convenient book format. I highly recommend having one on hand for your journey.

London Hiker

http://londonhiker.com

Catherine Redfern runs the London Hiker website, and has created two fantastic online resources to help you plan a long-distance walk: Trail Walking for First Timers, a three week e-course, and Walk Your Weekends, a multimedia guide to Catherine's top 14 weekend walking getaways in Britain. If you live in the UK and are interested in Walk Your Weekends, you'll want to purchase that, as Trail Walking for First Timers is included in WYW. Both are affordably priced, at £19.99 and £47.

National Trails Website

http://www.nationaltrail.co.uk/

This is the official website for the fifteen National Trails of England and Wales and has trail information, trail news, and tips on planning your walk. You can also request a certificate of completion after you walk the Ridgeway.

Events on the Ridgeway

https://www.nationaltrail.co.uk/en_GB/trails/the-ridgeway/events/

If you don't want your Ridgeway journey to coincide with other events (like a cycling, walking, or running race) then be sure to check online before you book your walk. The big ones are the Race to the Stones (which is usually in early to mid July), The Ridgeway Challenge 86 Miles (late August), and The Century to the Stones (which I coincided with in September).

Rambling Man

https://ramblingman.org.uk/walks/ridgeway/

This is a blog written by Andrew Bowden, who chronicles a seven-day walk of the Ridgeway, split into various weekends. He is also, coincidentally, Catherine Redfern's (of London Hiker) other half. Andrew's blog is what helped me to originally decide to walk the Ridgeway. His perspective is also good if you're thinking of walking the trail in weekends rather than all at once, as I did. You can read his experience on his blog, or you can purchase the ebook online.

ON THE PODCAST

The Into the Woods podcast is about personal growth through outdoor adventures.

You can find Holly's show on Apple Podcasts, or wherever you listen to podcasts. Links to subscribe, as well as the full list of episodes, can be found here:

http://www.hollyworton.com/podcast/

The following episodes may be of interest to you. Most of the episodes below have downloadable transcripts (no email required to get the pdf)—or you can read the transcript online in the show notes.

- 396 Jane Talbot ~ How to Improve Your Sports Mindset
- 395 Holly Worton ~ How to Know When to Quit Your Adventures
- 393 Holly Worton ~ Staying Safe in the Outdoors
- 386 Heather Waring ~ Walking for Personal Development and Self Care
- 383 Anne Malambo ~ How Solo Travel Can Change Our Lives

- 382 Holly Worton ~ Know Your Why For Your Outdoor Adventures
- 376 Holly Worton ~ Long Distance Walks: Time and Space to Think and Reflect
- 368 Yvette Webster ~ How to Take Your Hiking to the Next Level
- 359 Adam Wells ~ How To Prepare For Your First Long Distance Trail
- 354 Stephen Marriott ~ The Life-changing Magic of Walking a Long-Distance Trail

ABOUT THE AUTHOR

Holly Worton is an author and podcaster who helps people get to know themselves better through connecting with Nature, so they can feel happier and more fulfilled. Holly enjoys spending time outdoors. She loves trail running, walking long-distance trails and exploring Britain's sacred sites. She's originally from California and now lives in England's Surrey Hills, but she has also lived in Spain, Costa Rica, Mexico, Chile, and Argentina. Holly is a member of the Druid order OBOD.

Podcast

You can find her podcast on Apple Podcasts, or wherever you listen to podcasts. Links to subscribe, as well as the full list of episodes, can be found here:

    http://www.hollyworton.com/podcast/

Patreon

You can support her work and get access to her ebooks by joining her on Patreon:

https://www.patreon.com/hollyworton

Books

You can find her other work—including her books on business mindset, nature, and walking long-distance trails—wherever you purchased this title.

Newsletter

Finally, you can stay in touch by subscribing to her newsletter on her main website:

http://www.hollyworton.com/

amazon.com/author/hollyworton
facebook.com/HollyWortonPage
twitter.com/hollyworton
instagram.com/hollyworton
goodreads.com/HollyWorton
bookbub.com/profile/holly-worton

ALSO BY HOLLY WORTON

Walking books

Alone on the South Downs Way: A Tale of Two Journeys from Winchester to Eastbourne

Walking the Downs Link: Planning Guide & Reflections on Walking from St. Martha's Hill to Shoreham-by-Sea

Walking the Wey-South Path: Planning Guide & Reflections on Walking from Guildford to Amberley

Nature books

If Trees Could Talk: Life Lessons from the Wisdom of the Woods

If Trees Could Talk: Life Lessons from the Wisdom of the Woods — A Companion Workbook

Into the Woods Short Reads

How to Add More Adventure to Your Life

How to Practice Self-Love: Actual Steps You Can Take To Love Yourself More

How to Practice Self Care: Even When You Think You're Too Busy

How to Develop Your Own Inner Compass: Learn to Trust Yourself and Easily Make the Best Decisions

Into the Woods Short Reads: Box Set Books 1-5

Business Mindset series

Business Beliefs: Upgrade Your Mindset to Overcome Self Sabotage, Achieve Your Goals, and Transform Your Business (and Life)

Business Beliefs: A Companion Workbook

Business Blocks: Transform Your Self-Sabotaging Mind Gremlins, Awaken Your Inner Mentor, and Allow Your Business Brilliance to Shine

Business Blocks: A Companion Workbook

Business Visibility: Mindset Shifts to Help You Stop Playing Small, Dimming Your Light and Devaluing Your Magic

Business Visibility: A Companion Workbook

Business Intuition: Tools to Help You Trust Your Own Instincts, Connect with Your Inner Compass, and Easily Make the Right Decisions

Business Intuition: A Companion Workbook

Business Mindset Books: Box Set Books 1-4

Personal growth

The Year You Want: Imagine Your Best Life and Design Your Ideal Year, So You Don't Leave Your Life to Chance

Workcations: Laser Focused Getaways for Massive Productivity (Do More in Less Time to Achieve Your Goals and Enjoy Life)

En español

Si los árboles hablaran: enseñanzas de vida desde la sabiduría de los árboles

El año que quieres: imagina la vida que deseas y planea tu año ideal, para no dejarlos al azar

REVIEW TEAM

Would you like to be a part of my review team?

I really value the feedback and reviews I get from my readers. They make a huge difference in helping me (and other authors) reach new people. I know that it takes time to read and review a book, and I value the time people put into this. Thank you so much!

Here's what's involved....

Advance Review Copies

Whenever I have a new book coming out, I will send you an email to see if you would like to get an advance ebook copy for review on Amazon and/or Goodreads (or elsewhere online!).

If you are able to write an honest review by the deadline (I'll let you know about the timeline), then I'll send over a copy for you to read before it's on sale to the general public.

I can also send you free copies of any of my existing books (ebooks or audio) if you'd like to review them.

Audiobooks

If you enjoy audiobooks, I can also provide free audiobook codes so you can listen to the new audiobooks and review online. I don't produce all of my books as audiobooks, but I will offer you codes for the ones that are available.

Your review

If you enjoy the book, please post your review on Amazon.com or your local Amazon.

You can also post reviews on the online bookstores, social media, your blog, and anywhere else you feel like sharing. Amazon is the biggie for online reviews, but Goodreads, Instagram, and other online outlets all help.

Unsubscribe

This is a simple email list, so if you change your mind about being involved for whatever reason, you can unsubscribe from the list at any time.

Join now

If you would like to join, please fill out the form on my website and then look out for an email confirmation. Learn more here: https://www.hollyworton.com/review-team/.

HOLLY'S GROVE

I'd love for you to join me in my private community for readers, Patrons, clients, and students only. It's a place to talk about tree communication and outdoors adventures. You can ask any questions if you have them.

I'll also be sharing updates about my upcoming book projects and launches.

This is a general group, so we'll be talking both trees and outdoors adventures—and all the stuff I write about.

I'd love to get to know you in there!

You can find it here:
http://hollyworton.com/grove

A REQUEST

If you enjoyed this book, please review it online. It takes just a couple of minutes to write a quick review. It would mean the world to me! Good reviews help other readers to discover new books.

Thank you, thank you, thank you.